Thriving Through Change

A Leader's Practical Guide to Change Mastery

Elaine Biech

Alexandria, VA

12 11 10 09 08 07 1 2 3 4 5 6 7 8

ASTD Press is an internationally renowned source of insightful and practical information on workplace learning and performance topics, including training basics, evaluation and return-on-investment, instructional systems development, e-learning, leadership, and career development.

Ordering information: Books published by ASTD Press can be purchased by visiting our website at store.astd.org or by calling 800.628.2783 or 703.683.8100.

Library of Congress Control Number: 2006932490

ISBN-10: 1-56286-464-5
ISBN-13: 978-1-56286-464-4

ASTD Press Editorial Staff:

Director: Cat Russo
Manager, Acquisitions & Author Development: Mark Morrow
Editorial Manager: Jacqueline Edlund-Braun
Editorial Assistant: Kelly Norris
Retail Trade Specialist: Nancy Silva

Copyeditor: Alfred F. Imhoff
Indexer: April Michelle Davis
Proofreader: Kris Patenaude
Interior Design and Production: Kathleen Schaner
Cover Design: Kristi Sone
Cover Illustration: Todd Davidson

Printed by Victor Graphics Inc., Baltimore, MD, www.victorgraphics.com

For Shane and Thad—
two guys who changed my life forever

Contents

Appendixes

Preface

A multitude of books have been written about change by many very smart people. So why one more? Why this book? Change *is* the reason. Change is happening so quickly that it is almost impossible to keep up with the changes—let alone implement them! Change agents and leaders of change are under pressure to produce—and they need—a practical model, supported by useful tools that they can use immediately. Change leaders need a resource that

- is practical and easy to implement
- provides a map to guide them through a multitude of responsibilities
- addresses the diverse roles they must perform.

That's what this book delivers in hundreds of practical ways. It features

- a commonsense, comprehensive model to implement change
- change management steps that are easy to understand—with tasks you can actually perform
- lists of optional implementation ideas—with many choices, because your organization is different from others
- dozens of tools—old tools; new tools; tools to help you generate, organize, and decide
- theories, models, and history—not too many, but enough to remind you of why you do what you do
- techniques to hone your skills—after all, change agents and leaders also need to change and improve
- activities you can implement—23 ready-to-deliver activities to facilitate and lead change
- an employee's success guide—help for the people who really make change happen.

Every change is different, requiring change leaders and change agents to play different roles. A change agent needs to be

- both a carpenter and a conductor, knowing when to build and when to direct
- both a mystic and a mechanic, knowing how to produce a miracle and how to make a repair

- both a wing walker and a trapeze artist, knowing when to hang on and when to let go
- both a farmer and a musician, knowing when to sow alone and when to align for harmony.

As you perform all the roles expected of you, you will feel fulfilled as well as frustrated, exhilarated as well as exasperated. This is natural. This book will help you fulfill all your roles by providing logical lists and implementable ideas. And the book will also help you understand the emotional roller coaster by offering solid advice and plans leading to success.

This book is grounded in theory yet also chock-full of practical, real-world change management techniques. It provides you with skills and knowledge to play all the roles required to implement successful change initiatives. It was designed to enhance your competencies.

As I work with clients around the world to assess, design, develop, implement, and evaluate change initiatives, I find myself inventing models, pulling tools from old books, and scrambling to put words on paper that will answer my clients' immediate needs. This book brings many of those tools and tactics together under one model that utilizes just six straightforward steps. And the book also features practical and provocative activities for you and your change teams, winning ideas to further your learning, and a success (rather than survival) guide for your employees.

You will learn that change isn't fast, cheap, or easy but is constant and here to stay. I hope this book will become your companion on this exciting journey we call change!

Elaine Biech
May 2007

Acknowledgments

Every author needs a flight crew to launch a new book. ASTD and its consultants provide the support for a smooth flight. It was first class from takeoff to landing. Thank you to

- Cat Russo, publisher, for creating a synergistic climate in which the publishing team excels and authors have a safe flight.
- Mark Morrow, editor, for trusting me with this important task and for providing deadlines for a smooth landing.
- Jacki Edlund-Braun, editorial manager, for coordinating the complex process that enabled the manuscript to take wing as a bound book.
- Alfred Imhoff, copyeditor and word traffic controller, who managed my stray sentence structure, prodded my prepositions into place, and corrected capitalization.

Thank you, Lorraine and Dan, for managing the office and keeping things in shape while I wrote. It was a first-class flight.

Thanks, too, to all the authors, consultants, experts, and gurus who, like me, are trying to provide tools and models to make change a more pleasant experience: Geoff Bellman, Peter Block, William Bridges, Dan Cohen, Daryl Conner, Jeff Evans, Ann Gilley, Rosabeth Moss Kanter, John Kotter, Jim Kouzes, Pat McLagan, David Nadler, Jeff Russell, Chuck Schaefer, Peter Senge, David Ulrich, Marvin Weisbord, Margaret Wheatley, and the hundreds of change agents working in this new arena.

We're all working for a better world and a renewed tomorrow. And we're going to succeed!

Part I

Getting Ready for a Change

Chapter 1

Changing Times

Security is mostly a superstition. It does not exist in nature. Avoiding danger is no safer in the long run than outright exposure. Life is either a daring adventure or nothing.

—Helen Keller

In This Chapter:

- Signposts of change
- Defining the moment of change
- Managing change
- Myths of change
- Change ain't easy
- Plan of the book

Change—ever present, ever accelerating. Consider a couple of examples. In the 1700s, a stagecoach traveled comfortably at 10 miles an hour. The steam engine was invented in the 1800s and could carry people at almost 20 miles an hour. The rate of speed doubled in 100 years. Less than a century later, airplanes flew at 100 miles an hour, quadrupling the rate of speed. In less than 50 years, manned planes such as the SR-71 and the X-15 (rocket) were flying in excess of Mach 3 (three times the speed of sound, more than 2,000 miles an hour). Today you can outfly the sun, having breakfast in New York and then again in San Diego the same morning—not that you would want to!

Consider knowledge—a topic closely related to change. How quickly does current world knowledge change? In the past knowledge doubled from A.D. 1 to 1500, or in 1,500 years. It doubled again from 1500 to 1800, in 300 years. It doubled again from 1800 to 1900, in 100 years. By 1940, the doubling rate was every 20 years. And by 1970, it was seven years. Today, it is estimated that knowledge doubles every one to two years. It is predicted that by 2020, our collective body of knowledge will double every 72 days. For example, I "Googled" (a new word—another sign of change) "organizational change," and the search uncovered 52,130,000 sites. The number of sites will have changed—perhaps doubled—by the time you read this!

We are certainly an information-rich society. More than 1 million new websites are created every day. One weekly issue of the *New York Times* contains more information than the average person was likely to come across in a lifetime in the 17th century.

What does this mean to you personally? Do you know someone who is in college? It is estimated that half the facts learned in engineering while in college will be obsolete five years after graduation. Half of what is learned in computer science will be outdated in just two years. And the same is true in nearly every field, because information is changing, accelerating at an almost incomprehensible rate.

The accelerating rate of information is directly related to the accelerating rate of change. This means more decisions and an increased number of choices. Have you tried to make a simple purchase for your home lately? Technology has changed, requiring many more decisions than you had just a few years ago. How many decisions did you have to make when you purchased a telephone 15 years ago? Probably very few. How many decisions do you need to make today when you purchase a telephone? Camera? Television? Let's consider the decisions for each:

- *Telephone:* Land line or cell? Caller ID? Digital answering? Speaker phone? Voice-activated dialing? Camera phone? Internet capable? Bluetooth capable? Video and music capable? Global Positioning System? Personal digital assistant combination? Text messaging? Picture messaging? Which carrier? What plan? How many minutes? Free minutes? Carrier-to-carrier plan? Family plan? Replacement phones? Warranties? Insurance? Ringer choices? Battery life? Headset? Charger? Car charger? Other accessories? And most important, what color?
- *Camera:* Traditional single-lens reflex or digital? Number of pixels? Optical/digital zoom lens? 3x? 10x? Internal memory? Removable memory size? Computer compatibility? How will you download the pictures? Battery type? Rechargeable? Backup battery pack?

How large is the storage capability? Warranty? Size of the picture viewing frame? Waterproof? Available attachments? Carrying case? Photo lens? Reputation for reliability? How cool is it (status)? Where to buy? Online? What about a video camera that can take snapshots? Or do you just want to stay with the disposables you've been using?

- *Television:* Flat screen? Plasma? High definition? HD-ILA? Digital? DLP? LCD? Rear projection? Traditional? Resolution? Dual HDMI high definition input? 3HDMI? Built in DVR? Recording time? Screen size? Accessory compatibility? Built in VCR or DVD? Integrated PC input? Stereo? Home theater? Speaker system? Surround sound? Direct TV? Satellite?

And there will be many more changes between the time I write this chapter and you read it. Changing something as personal and as simple as a camera may require weeks of research, with changes occurring right before your eyes.

Even purchasing my favorite breakfast cereal, Cheerios, has changed. I like Cheerios—the big yellow box with a heart-shaped bowl on the front filled with those crunchy round ohs. Today there are a dozen kinds of Cheerios from which to select: honey nut or multigrain; fruity Cheerios or yogurt burst Cheerios (vanilla or strawberry); or berry burst Cheerios in berry burst triple berry, berry burst strawberry, or berry burst strawberry banana. A mind-boggling sea of information is ready for you as you prepare to make decisions and changes of almost every kind.

Like your personal life, organizational life is changing. The accelerating rate of information produces an accelerated rate of change. Driven by global competition, shifting workforce demographics, customer requirements, regulatory pressures, technology advancements, stockholder expectations, and a host of other events, organizations must produce rapid change. The organization may be looking for change to enable it to adjust its mission, transform its identity, improve the quality of its products or services, decrease the amount of time it takes to get products to market, or meet a number of other goals.

We live in changing times. There is no doubt about it. The increased amount of information and speed at which we can access information have placed organizations on ever-accelerating paths of change.

Signposts of Change

Change is both a journey and a destination. As you travel the change route, you will meet many people with many attitudes about change. Think of these views as signposts; just as a signpost directs you to a destination on a journey, so your attitude about change directs your attitude about the outcome of change. For example, people may see change as:

- *Normal and expected.* You may feel that change happens naturally; people grow, organizations grow. You realize that change will occur naturally. Change happens all the time.
- *New and exciting.* You may feel that change means growth and new beginnings. As in the quote from Helen Keller at the beginning of this chapter, change means adventure, and without change life may be boring. Change is opportunity-rich.
- *Difficult and worthwhile.* Your attitude is that it isn't going to be easy and will require work. You have a "no pain, no gain" philosophy. In the end, you know most things are better for change.
- *Daunting but necessary.* This is similar to the previous attitude, but with a stronger emphasis on "hard work." You may feel that change is a major event that requires a huge investment. However, you also recognize that it can't be ignored if an organization is to continue to grow and develop.

Even with slight nuances, all these are healthy attitudes toward change. Because change is here to stay, that's good. Unfortunately, all people do not have the same healthy attitudes. Some people may deny, refuse, resist, defy, fight, stonewall, or sabotage change. Some people are downright hostile. Theories abound that suggest that these reactions are based in anger or fear. Whatever the case may be, it is certain that change carries emotional attachments—often due to past experiences.

When organizations know change is coming, they can plan for change more easily and can help their employees adjust to and accept change more readily. Organizations have begun to appreciate the importance of the human element during change, much like the comprehensive approach proposed by the total quality expert W. Edwards Deming.

This book proposes a process with signposts along the way to guide leaders and change agents through the total change process. It includes involving the workforce and addressing reactions to change.

Defining the Moment of Change

What is change? When does change happen? Think about your personal life. Change is happening to you all the time. Sometimes change happens so naturally that you don't notice the subtle shifts. For example, are you aware that your stomach lining changes every three days to protect itself from the acidity of its digestive juices?

At other times, a single event can instantly change your life forever. The same is true in organizations. Change can come in small shifts to make incremental improvements, or in one tremendous upheaval that establishes an entirely new organization. Like change in your personal life, change in organizations is both an ending and a beginning. It can bring joy and sorrow, satisfaction and discontent all at once.

In the Chinese language, the word "crisis" is composed of two characters. One represents danger and the other represents opportunity. Change, which is sometimes crisis driven, has the same positive/negative relationship. There is danger in change, but there is also huge opportunity. It is the manager's job to identify the opportunity and the path to the opportunity.

Managing Change

Managing change is a complex task required of all leaders in today's rapidly changing world. Guiding the task is difficult, because unlike the simple (did I say simple?) task of purchasing a camera, in an organization, a huge number of decisions must be made. All these decisions work together in a system. Changing one thing in the system affects many other parts of it.

Managing change effectively is the single most important element in organizational success. Unfortunately, organizations have not always been successful in this area. Some experts suggest a failure rate of more than 50 percent. Part of the reason is that past research has not identified what is required to make change successful. Without a map to guide them, many organizations have plotted their own courses. In addition, leaders have not given change management the attention it requires.

Winning Idea:

To learn more about change in organizations, read the series of four articles about change written by Patricia McLagan that appeared in the November and December 2002 and January and February 2003 issues of ASTD's *T+D*. They are also referenced in several places in this book.

Managers sometimes feel caught in the middle. They may have had input about the change—or not. They may think it is a good thing to do—or not. In any case, they are responsible for taking the organization's position and making it work.

This book takes the complex task of managing organizational change and breaks it down into manageable steps. Although it does not tell you everything to do within those steps, it does remind you of the questions you must ask along the way.

Myths of Change

Leaders cannot naively rush into a change effort without some very basic knowledge of systems. They need to understand the basics of change and how to make an impact on the outcomes. They need to explore their closely held beliefs about change; are they true or myths? For example, is resistance a way of life during change, or can it be prevented? Does change require a strong leader who clearly defines the plan so that employees know what to do, or should the plan be flexible? Should a leader inform employees of an impending change before the details are worked out, or is it better to wait until there is more information?

Let's look at a few myths about change that many of us accept as true because they have become a part of the change folklore and our belief system.

The only constant is change: a myth. In *Built to Last,* Jim Collins and Jerry Porras state that "a visionary company almost religiously preserves its core ideology—changing seldom if ever. Core values in a visionary company form a rock-solid foundation and do not drift with the trends and fashions of the day." Some organizations' values have remained intact for well over a hundred years. In addition, the basic purpose of a visionary company can serve as a guiding beacon for centuries. However, maintaining their core ideologies does not stop organizations from a compelling drive toward progress. They will change and adapt without compromising their core ideals.

The conflict in a change effort should be avoided: a myth. Change by its very definition is a diversion from the status quo and will create a clash with the system as it currently exists. Conflict can be healthy, especially when it leads to a more positive change. It may bring out new ideas and nuances not considered while designing the change.

You can have a successful change effort without creating conflict: a myth. Effective change management recognizes that change is disruptive and naturally creates a tension between the "as-is" and the "to-be." Unfortunately, most organizations are not realistic about the amount of conflict that will occur as a result of the change. Leaders expect individuals to desire to operate in the best interests of the organizations or to easily see the merits of the change. Neither of these will occur without a great deal of preparation to avoid the collision between what is today and where the organization would like to be.

Given a choice, people want to be involved in the change that concerns them: a myth. Although most of us would like to believe that employees want to help design the change—want to be a part of the planning—the truth is that few do. Employees become nervous when asked to think of new ideas, concerned that they may look dumb when called upon to identify a new way to do things. They do not want to be placed in a position of risk. Instead of participating in a proactive way to initiate change, they prefer to be the victims of change. Eventually, however, they will jump on the bandwagon as they see the potential success of the design.

Change is good: a myth. "Change is good only if it adds value," states Pat McLagan in her series of articles in *T+D*. Change can be good if it is well thought out and has had adequate planning. An organization will be most successful if it adheres to its values and guiding principles when planning and implementing a change effort. It may not be good if the organization ignores these and is reacting to external pressures such as stockholders' demands for greater revenue or changing regulations. U.S. organizations do not have a very good track record with a success rate of less than 50 percent. Does this make change sound "good"?

Leaders who have passion for a change may fail because they do not appear professional: a myth. Unrestrained passion, like anything in excess, may pose an issue. But passionate enthusiasm for change motivates other employees. A leader's passion often inspires others, drawing them into the excitement side of change.

Employees will always resist change: a myth. Resistance may come from employees, and it may also come from senior management. However, resistance can be minimized and even eliminated when the human element of change has been addressed, ensuring adequate communication, addressing the WIIFMs (what's in it for me), and presenting individuals' roles in the new organization. People choose to change. If they have been given good reasons to change, they will not resist. As you read about change, you will find that many change experts list resistance to change as a barrier to success. Remember that organizations have a very powerful advantage to shape behavior and response by encouraging it, not forcing required behavior.

What other strongly held beliefs do you have about change that you may wish to explore before embarking on a change journey?

Change Ain't Easy

Why ain't change easy? First of all, leaders and organizations often need to recover from a poor track record on change. Employees may not have faith in their organizations when change has failed in the past. They may start out with a "here we go again" attitude. Second, organizations are complex entities, making change more difficult. Let's look briefly at each.

Poor track records on change. Statistics abound lamenting the poor success rates of change:

- The *McKinsey Quarterly* reported in June 2006 that only 30 percent of major change initiatives were reported to be at least mostly successful in preparing the organization for sustained performance.
- Half to two-thirds of major corporate change efforts are considered failures, as reported in *Breaking the Code of Change*, edited by Michael Beer and Nitin Nohria.

- The results of a Booz Allen Hamilton study states that 25 percent of all change projects are successful, 63 percent are cancelled, and 12 percent fail.
- According to Patricia McLagan in a *T+D* article, 65 percent of all changes are considered failures.
- Beer, Eisenstat, and Spector reported in the November–December 1990 *Harvard Business Review* that one-third of the change efforts actually made the situation worse! Statistics like these are scary.

Why the failure? There are several reasons. First, research tells us that it isn't working, but very little research tells us why. Second, leaders don't give change management the attention required, and only after failing can they see what they should have done—for example, "I thought I could delegate this down like other projects." And third, the field of organizational development (OD) is relatively young and thus has little data to support it.

The good news is that, first, academics recognize the importance of conducting research to determine what works and what doesn't and have started gathering and analyzing data. And second, more leaders are aware of their responsibilities for making a change management initiative work. When asked what they would do differently, most leaders say they would develop a plan and stick with it. Third, OD practitioners are getting on the change management research bandwagon, and it will not be long before we are inundated with data that supports what works and what doesn't.

Stability in organizations being viewed as excellence. Over the years, we have learned how to design organizations for stability. We have done a great job of ensuring that everything is flawless and running perfectly. Processes are within control. Products are within tolerance. Budgets have procedures. Roles and responsibilities are clearly defined. Managers are coached to write good objectives that meet the goals on the balanced scorecard. Employees are hired, trained, and compensated for meeting the objectives in their performance plans. Everything is designed to run smoothly. Taming chaos and eliminating surprises are the mantra. When these characteristics, both the people and the systems, operate together, they form an organization with all the enduring qualities that define it as *the* organization.

All this stability adds complexity, but it also solidifies the organization so that change becomes very difficult. When we make a change in one part of the system, it will affect many of the other parts of the system as well. We have done a great job of designing stable organizations.

Consider one small aspect of change. Say that one of your key people, Mason, has been doing a job a certain way. Not only has Mason been doing it a particular way, but he has trained everyone in the department to do it the same way. He has been recognized for doing the job the same way for 12 years. You tell him that things have changed. He is not to do it that particular way any longer. He is to do it the new way. Mason says, "But I've been doing it this way for 12 years. I have a plaque that says you want me to do it this way! I've trained all these people to do it this way! You have given me bonuses to do it this way!" Mason cannot accept that he has been wrong for 12 years. Therefore the new way must be wrong.

Now multiply Mason and his department by all the departments in an organization and multiply that by all the processes in the company and multiply that by all changes that organizations are facing for the future.

The good news is that many people are interested in learning more about change. People like you who are reading books like this one recognize the bumpy road to change.

There are other reasons why change ain't easy, but let's save those for another chapter. Change is an ever-present part of our lives, and it is not going to go away. Take whatever change you've been through the past couple of years and multiply it by a factor of two for next year. Change is here to stay.

Plan of the Book

This book presents you with a practical approach and tools that will lighten your load and make your change journey easier. In the next two chapters, we'll look generally at how to facilitate change and various models of how to undertake a change effort. Then we'll look at each aspect of a six-step model for a change effort that I've found particularly helpful. Finally, we'll look at the big picture and the future of change-oriented organizations. Throughout the book, there are sidebars featuring winning ideas to consider, as well as many illustrations, tables, lists, and worksheets to make the topics more accessible and practical to implement.

Chapter 2

Facilitating Change

If there is any one secret of success, it lies in the ability to get the other person's point of view and see things from his angle as well as from your own.
—Henry Ford

In This Chapter:

- Change management roles
- Change agent skill assessment
- The other half of the job: facilitating
- Quick-start advice for the change agent

Change won't happen by itself. Just as you can plan a trip, someone must eventually decide when to start, what to pack, where to go, and how to get there. When implementing change, this role lies with the change agent, change facilitator, or the leader, depending upon the size of the organization, the size of the change, and the design for implementing the change. This chapter focuses on facilitating the organizational change effort—initiating the "trip."

After a brief examination of the roles required for the change journey, this chapter addresses the skills needed by the change agent. These skills are focused in two areas: the ability to complete the steps found in the model of change that I present in this book, and the skills required by a proficient facilitator. We'll start looking at the change model I've developed in chapter 3; for now, suffice it to say that it involves an easy-to-remember progression of six steps: challenge, harmonize, activate, nurture, guide, and evaluate—spelling out C-H-A-N-G-E.

Change Management Roles

Differentiating change management roles is unique to every organization. There is no right or wrong title. It is more important to clarify who has which roles. The lists of responsibilities for the leader and change agent given in table 2-1 is a general overview.

Additional responsibilities may be added to both sides. In some cases, an organization may choose to swap out responsibilities for a variety of reasons. For example, at the department level or in small organizations, the leader and the change agent may be one and the same. In general, the leader must be able to create a sense of urgency and the vision for the preferred future and be committed beyond the end. The change agent must be able to develop and facilitate the implementation and be credible to the workforce. The leader answers the what and why; the change agent answers the how and when.

One action that is sure to lead to disaster is if the leader abdicates all roles to the change agent. The workforce must see that the leader is committed to

Table 2-1. Change Management Responsibilities

Leader/Sponsor	Change Agent/Facilitator
Develops the vision Provides input to the business case Establishes a sense of urgency Shows credible and unwavering commitment Displays endorsement in actions and words Removes barriers in the system Responds to emerging issues Directs the change implementation team Communicates the vision constantly Supports actions addressing reactions Approves metrics Holds others accountable to attain metrics Delivers implementation plan Holds others accountable to implement Supports practices to institutionalize change Implements rewards and consequences Stays the course	Collects and analyzes data Measures organizational readiness Builds a business case Coaches the leadership Recommends implementation team members Facilitates teams and coaches team leaders Prepares implementation plans Recommends strategies and methods Coordinates implementation Ensures milestones are met Designs communication plans Addresses reactions to change Recommends metrics Conducts risk assessment Identifies and exploits short-term wins Evaluates the change effort Identifies rewards and consequences Creates plan for change-ready organization

the effort. If the change agent is doing it all, it signals a lack of commitment and sounds the death knell for the effort.

Sometimes we get hung up on nomenclature. Is it really a change leader or a change sponsor? Or maybe the person is a champion. Is the implementer a change agent or a facilitator? Or a change advocate? Or is the leader the advocate? Though all these roles exist, someone is driving the bus, and in some cases it may be a shared responsibility. In this chapter, we call the person(s) driving the bus the change agent. But the name of the role doesn't matter. Don't let the terminology prevent you from appreciating an important role.

It all needs to be done. Initiate a discussion between the leaders and the change agent to ensure clarity of roles and responsibilities.

Winning Idea:

Purchase a copy of Ann Gilley's book *The Manager as Change Leader* and give it to your leaders. You will read more about the leadership role throughout chapters 4 through 9. Ann's book inspired the leader's VIEW that you'll read more about in chapter 5.

Change Agent Skill Assessment

The change management skills assessment in worksheet 2-1 identifies the skills required to move an organization through the change journey (an image of this worksheet is given here, and the reader can find a full-size version in appendix D and a PDF version on the companion CD-ROM. Be sure to complete this assessment, being honest with yourself. Your answers will guide you in the direction of the further learning you require.

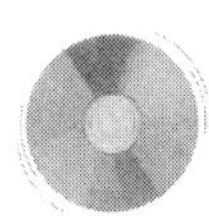

The 27 questions in worksheet 2-1 are essentially a list of the tasks completed by the change agent when using the CHANGE Model. There is no good or bad score. Once you have completed the assessment, go back again and determine which tasks are your responsibility. You may wish to use a highlighter to mark those for which you are accountable. Now do a quick comparison. Identify any skills that you have both highlighted (your responsibility) and you have scored average, a 3, or lower. Place an X in front of these, because these are the ones you probably want to develop first.

These suggestions will help you start your development:

1. Identify the areas in worksheet 2-1 that have the most Xs—those that are both your responsibility and that you have scored a 3 or less.
2. Read the chapter that corresponds to each CHANGE step. Here's a quick reference:
   - Challenge the current state (Step 1), chapter 4
   - Harmonize and align leadership (Step 2), chapter 5
   - Activate commitment (Step 3), chapter 6
   - Nurture and formalize a design (Step 4), chapter 7
   - Guide implementation (Step 5), chapter 8
   - Evaluate and institutionalize the change (Step 6), chapter 9.

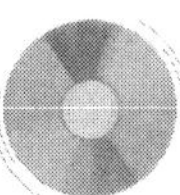

Worksheet 2-1. Change Management Skills Assessment

Here's an opportunity to rate your competency in each of the six CHANGE Model steps.

Use this 1–5 rating scale: 1 = no experience or skill; 2 = minimal ability; 3 = average ability; 4 = above-average ability; 5 = outstanding ability.

Challenge the current state:

__ Use a process to gather and analyze data.
__ Build a business case.
__ Implement actions to establish a sense of urgency.
__ Differentiate change management roles.
__ Determine organizational readiness for change.

Harmonize and align leadership:

__ Build trust and confidence in diverse people at all levels of the organization.
__ Select and build a change implementation team.
__ Coach change leaders about the required leadership qualities.
__ Facilitate a process to create a compelling change vision.
__ Design a communication plan.

Activate commitment:

__ Attain buy-in to the vision.
__ Design an implementation based on solid theory.
__ Define and predict reactions to change.
__ Build critical mass.

Nurture and formalize a design:

__ Implement actions that address systems issues.
__ Use a process to select appropriate metrics.
__ Conduct a risk assessment.
__ Use a variety of implementation and planning tools.

Guide implementation:

__ Foster collaboration between diverse groups.
__ Utilize organizational politics positively.
__ Identify motivational factors for various individuals.
__ Use short-term gains to build momentum.
__ Coordinate numerous and varied activities ensuring that timelines are met.

Evaluate and institutionalize the change:

__ Create a process to evaluate the change effort.
__ Identify ways to institutionalize the change.
__ Compare the organizational culture to the change results.
__ Create a change-ready organization.

3. Turn to appendix C and identify the recommended reading for each chapter. Add more to your knowledge base with this content.
4. Identify and read the *Infolines* related to the topics listed in appendix C.
5. Read the exercises in chapter 11 that correspond to the areas that you would like to develop further.
6. Register for ASTD's Facilitating Organizational Change Certificate Program.
7. Use your network to identify additional resources.

The Other Half of the Job: Facilitating

Understanding the elements in a change initiative is a basic starting point. The change agent also requires several other important competencies to be successful. Two other areas include change leadership skills (process skills, people skills, business acumen, and political/cultural savvy) and facilitation skills.

Change Leadership Skills

Consider the following change leadership skills required by a change agent to support the change effort. If you do not rate an A for all these, you may want to draw on others in the leadership ranks as support.

Process skills:

- Comfortable with data and statistics
- Implements problem-solving techniques
- Comprehends vital business processes
- Understands customer and supplier processes
- Practices continuous process improvement.

People skills:

- Good communicator: verbal and written
- Effective listener
- Builds relationships with others
- Fosters collaboration among diverse people
- Ability to observe and interpret nonverbal cues
- Understands and applies concepts of group dynamics.

Business acumen:

- Comprehends internal and external customer and supplier relationships
- Works with decision makers at all levels
- Knowledgeable of the organization's priorities
- Values measurement to focus attention
- Experienced with sharing information across all levels.

Political/cultural savvy:

- Able to influence internal resources
- Utilizes internal politics to influence decisions
- Ally of informal leaders
- Applies meaning to organizational history and cultural norms
- Uses structure appropriately without being controlled by it.

Facilitation Skills for the Change Agent

A facilitator structures and guides participation in the change effort to make the work easier. Therefore, you'll most likely want to polish your facilitation skills. How many of these skills and/or tools are you able to implement?

- *Communication:* asking questions, paraphrasing, probing, including quieter people, summarizing, nonverbal communication, giving and receiving feedback, active listening.
- *Generating and organizing ideas:* brainstorming, affinity diagrams, matrix charts, flowcharts, round robin technique, cause-and-effect diagrams, creativity techniques.
- *Prioritizing and evaluating:* multi-voting, force field analysis, decision matrix, ranking and prioritizing, nominal group technique.

- *Making decisions:* Reaching a consensus, solving problems, decision-making strategies.
- *Meeting management:* using icebreakers; capturing ideas; establishing and complying with ground rules; using flipcharts, agendas, and note taking; implementing on-the-spot agendas; directing comments; maintaining focus; encouraging divergent views; managing conflict.
- *Teamwork:* writing team charters, identifying team strengths, monitoring task and maintenance behaviors, dealing with difficult team members.

Winning Idea:
You need to know all the nuances about change. You also need to be skilled as a facilitator. Obtain facilitator training to hone your skills. Or read one of the books listed in appendix C. I am partial to Fran Rees's *The Facilitator Excellence Handbook.*

Icebreakers are fun, and they help to get a meeting off to a good start. They are also fabulous tools for helping team members get to know each other better. When team members know each other as people, it is easier to work together. Table 2-2 lists quick team activities that you can use as openers at team meetings.

During meetings, you also keep the team moving and focused. You may use some of these interventions:

- *Provide information.* "The next step in the CHANGE Model is to select appropriate metrics."
- *Make suggestions.* "I suggest you take a break and finish this discussion when you return."
- *Provide feedback.* "We're halfway through the meeting and only three team members have spoken."
- *Ask questions.* "Do you see any patterns in the data that we should consider before leaving this page?"

Table 2-2. List of Team Warm-Ups

- For fun, I like to . . .
- If I could be any animal, I would be ____________________ because . . .
- My dream vacation is . . .
- The last book I read was . . .
- On Saturdays, I usually . . .
- The turning point in my life was . . .
- I feel best when people . . .
- Five things I want to do in the next five years include . . .
- One thing I recently learned on the job is . . .
- The slogan on my favorite T-shirt says . . .
- Something you may not know about me is . . .
- I once won a . . .
- To me, change means . . .

- *Lead team-building activities.* "Before we move on, let's go around the table and state what we did well while solving that problem and what we could have done better."
- *Reframe beliefs.* "Let's talk about what it means to withhold feedback from another department."
- *Remain silent.*

In addition to all the skills listed here—and there are a lot—chapter 4 introduces 24 characteristics that make a good facilitator.

Quick-Start Advice for the Change Agent

Be sure that the change leads to value. Is there a demand from the outside (regulation, customer satisfaction, shareholder demand) or the inside (new competencies, retirements)? Do unmet opportunities exist? Do conflicts exist about the future? Does the organization require a clear vision for the future?

Attain leadership support early. There may always be an excuse for delaying leadership commitment. But every day of delay is a postponement of success. Better advice: Don't start until leaders are on board and ready to make a public commitment. Leaders may be skilled at running a business but not changing a business, so they may need help to formulate a vision, plan, and rationale. Help them.

Sustain leadership support to the end. A lack of sponsorship toward the end generally results in wasted resources. Too often, leaders pull back when they feel the initiative is taking off. But a change effort is like an airplane; if you throttle back just as it is taking off, it will crash. Leaders need to sustain their support to the end, not just until things seem to be going well.

Think, work, dream, eat, and sleep communication. Keep the lines of communication open with all stakeholders. Open new lines of communication with those at all levels. You can never have too much support from too many areas. That means you cannot communicate too much. Communicate beyond the communication plan. Communicate beyond the boundaries of the immediate change initiative.

Maintain a holistic approach to the plan. Although this book breaks the change effort into six steps and divides those steps into substeps, every step in the process is related to every other step. You may think that you have finished with Step 1 in the model—Challenge the current state—once you are well into the second step, but you have not. You must constantly revisit completed actions. This is not because you didn't do a good job or didn't finish the job, but because approaching change holistically means that you must attend to changes created at every juncture. When you change one thing, it affects many others. Sustainable change requires monitoring and making additional changes as required.

Reach commitments for all resources before beginning. This assumes that you know the amount of money, time, and people required to complete the change. Give it your best shot. Don't be stingy. Don't be shy. Ask for what you need—all of it—and ensure that you have a full commitment for each aspect before the launch date.

Winning Idea:

Before your first change initiative, borrow or buy (you will eventually anyway!) Geoff Bellman's *The Consultant's Calling* and read chapter 9, "What Works When Creating Change." Bellman writes so eloquently that I could never do him justice in a summary.

Promote camaraderie among change agents. Generally, you will be working with an implementation team that guides the effort. In addition, you will be working with other cross-department team leaders who may develop or conduct portions of the intricate design work for specific areas of the organization. Build a group of team leaders to support each other, share information and techniques, celebrate wins, generate new ideas, solve problems, and perhaps (rarely) lament together. You can do more than build support for the change initiative; you can break down department barriers and make inroads into the organization's culture for future change.

Be prepared for the difficult days. There will be at least a few during the change journey. Everyone will not make it to the end of the journey. That's to be expected. Your job is not to ensure that everyone goes along for the whole ride but that they go along because they know it is the right thing to do for the organization and they want to be a part of the preferred future. Respect those that leave—it's their choice.

Chapter 3

Models of Change

It is not the strongest of the species that survive, nor the most intelligent, but the one most responsive to change.
—Charles Darwin

The voyage of discovery lies not in seeking new horizons but in seeing with new eyes.
—Marcel Proust

In This Chapter:

- Theories, strategies, and models
- History of change design
- Ethical considerations
- Overview of the CHANGE Model

Reinvention, learning organizations, audacious goals, revolution, quantum change, total quality management, breakthrough thinking, horizontal organization, stretch goals, Lean Six Sigma—you can probably attach a prominent scholar's name to each of these well-recognized change initiatives that at one time or another were the darlings of change management professionals. All displayed some success. Some demonstrated more results than others.

Two keys to success are important for all change efforts:

1. You need to have a plan. The plan must translate the concepts into concrete steps so that employees can implement them.
2. You need to carry out the plan—all of it. Carrying out the plan requires getting everyone involved who has a stake in the change.

So you must plan the work and work the plan.

Theories, Strategies, and Models

When people are trained only in techniques, without understanding the theory behind them, they have difficulty applying them to anything beyond a specific situation. The variables that contribute to change management are too complex to remember a few techniques that apply to any change situation. Therefore, it is important to learn more about the theories, models, and strategies that drive your efforts. This section serves to introduce you to (or remind you of) several important theories, strategies, models, and approaches. The funnel shown in figure 3-1 helps to describe the hierarchy of the three.

Think of the top of the funnel as theories. Theories are hypothetical statements of what we believe will happen. They are not practical but are broad in meaning and present the possibilities. The next level in the funnel is strategies. Strategies take the theory down one level and create a framework for design, thus getting us closer to a practical level. Models provide a step-by-step process. Models are useful in explaining in generic terms what must be done. However, most organizations will need to adapt a model to their own approach. The CHANGE Model presented in this book will need to be adapted to your specific needs and situation. The following theories, strategies, models, and approaches may be useful in understanding the underpinnings of change.

Theories

Systems theory views an organization as a complex system with boundaries allowing input and output. The organizational system exists within a larger external environment that is constantly exerting pressure on its boundaries, an environment with which the organization must interact. Systems theory

Figure 3-1. From Theories to Approaches

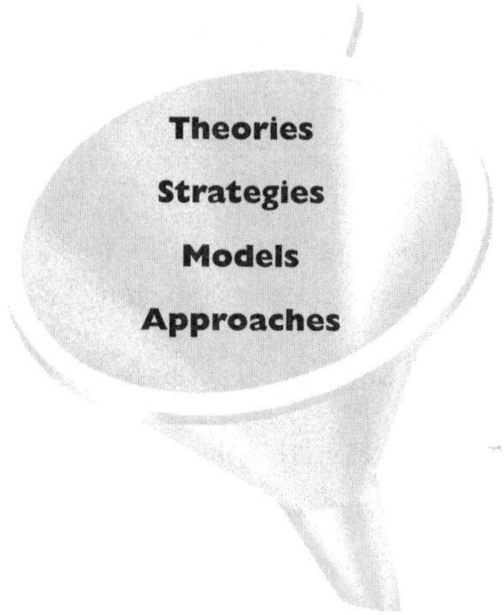

recognizes that a change in any part of the system creates change throughout the system. If one part of the system changes, other parts must change to accommodate this new system.

The organizational system is defined by its boundaries and internal structures. It is typically considered stable. The external environment is assumed to be in a state of continual flux. For example, if a purchasing department orders the same 1,000 sheets of glass from a supplier every month and the supplier increases prices, the change affects the entire system. To maintain profits, manufacturing reduces labor costs by changing production methods. Research may be tasked with developing a product that uses less glass, or purchasing may need to locate another supplier, or finance will pass along the price increase. One change creates changes in many other parts of the system.

Peter Senge, a leader in systems theory, presents a simple example. If one person is taking a shower and someone else in the same house (system) flushes the toilet, the water turns cold in the shower. The person in the shower may try to adjust the temperature. However, by the time he has adjusted the shower, the toilet bowl has filled, the water temperature goes back to normal, and the person in the shower will need to adjust the temperature again—this time making it cooler.

Theory E and *Theory O* are change management theories. The names of these theories were coined by the Harvard Business School professors Michael Beer and Nitin Nohria to describe two goals that drive change initiatives: near-term economic improvement or improvement in organizational capabilities. Theory E (for economic value) aims for a dramatic and rapid increase in shareholder value. It is driven from the top of the organization and makes use of outside consultants. Theory E relies heavily on cost cutting, downsizing, and asset sales to meet its objectives.

Conversely, Theory O (organizational capabilities) is a long-term approach that aims to create higher performance by fostering a powerful culture and capable workforce. It is characterized by high levels of employee participation and a flatter organizational structure. It attempts to build bridges between the organization and its employees, partially on the assumption that the involved employees will bond with the organization they have helped to change.

Chaos and Complexity Theory has its roots in the field of science. It is applied to organizations in an attempt to find order in the organizational environment. Purists would argue that combining the two terms "chaos" and "complexity" is incorrect because each represents a distinct theory from different disciplines.

In very simple terms, *Chaos Theory* is the study of how simple systems can generate complicated behavior. It recognizes that behavior in systems appears random but in fact reveals orderly patterns at deeper levels. In a business sense, it describes random, inherently unpredictable sequences over time.

Complexity Theory is the study of how complicated systems generate simple behavior. The assumption is that systems are interconnected or interwoven parts and that dynamic complexity exists in situations where cause and effects are subtle and effects over time are not obvious. In business, it admonishes us to *not* examine parts of the organizational system separately from the rest of the system.

Strategies

A strategy or a model for approaching change is a general design or plan for action. There are four generally accepted types of strategies:

- A facilitative strategy depends on a shared responsibility and the involvement of everyone in the organization.
- An informational strategy is based on delivering education or knowledge.
- An attitudinal strategy recognizes the need to change mindsets and, as a result, change behavior.
- Political strategies depend on giving, withholding, competing, or bargaining for scarce resources to accomplish the planned change's objectives.

Generally, change management efforts are most successful when they use a combination of the various types of strategies available. The CHANGE Model in this book uses an attitudinal basis, and it also relies on facilitative and informational approaches. Table 3-1 offers a comparison of the four types of strategies.

Models

Models—such as Kurt Lewin's Three-Step Model of unfreezing, change, and refreezing; Kotter's Eight-Step Model; and Nadler's Cycle of Change—

Table 3-1. Types of Strategies for Approaching Change

Type of Strategy	Rate of Implementation	Impact	Consequences	Acceptance Tactic
Facilitative	Faster	Surface	Short-term	Helping
Informational	Slower	In-depth	Long-term	Helping
Attitudinal	Slower	In-depth	Long-term	Persuading
Political	Faster	Surface	Short-term	Persuading

provide process guidance. Models generally demonstrate action and steps that flow from one to another. Models are road maps that offer guidance and cautions along the way.

Models are particularly useful for moving from your current state to your preferred future, offering steps in a generally sequential order—though, in practice, the steps are seldom perfectly linear. There will always be some overlap between steps. Change is rarely as linear a process as presented in any model.

Techniques, Approaches, and Frameworks

Techniques, approaches, and frameworks support a change model and may be used with the model as a tool to support one of the steps.

Appreciative Inquiry, though at times called a theory, is actually an approach to large-scale organizational change that involves the analysis of positive and successful (as opposed to negative) events. David Cooperrider is generally credited with developing the principles of Appreciative Inquiry. In typical problem solving, an organization identifies the problem, analyzes the causes, identifies possible solutions, and develops a plan. Yet Appreciative Inquiry identifies the best of "what is," envisions "what might be," discusses "what should be," and implements the "what will be," all from a positive, "appreciating" point of view. This approach also uses a basic framework called the 4-D model—discovery, dream, design, and destiny—to accomplish its objectives.

Action Research and Learning is both a model and a process. In its simplest form, it is a process whereby research or fact finding precedes action and follows it. The thought process looks something like this: fact finding—action—fact finding—action, and so on. The Action Research and Learning process takes shape as understanding increases. The process used in change management efforts remains focused on the desired state and how each systemic element needs to change.

Karl Albrecht's Change Response Cycle describes the four phases individuals work through when faced with change. The four phases are threat, problem, solution, and habit. Elisabeth Kubler-Ross was one of the first to recognize that humans go through phases following a loss. In her case, it was the families of dying cancer patients. Her five phases are denial, anger, bargaining, depression, and finally acceptance. You may see other forms of this, such as denial, resistance, adaptation, and involvement. All follow similar patterns that describe the phases people go through as they adjust to change. People perceive change as a loss—if only as the loss of what was.

Understanding organizational culture is important because it can be managed. The culture—represented by a shared set of symbols, values, beliefs, underlying assumptions, rewards, preferences, supporting policies, and dozens of other elements—can be changed by changing the elements that created it in the first place. Changing the culture—or at least adjusting it—changes the behavior of individuals. That is why it is important to introduce new symbols, celebrations, language, and rituals into the system to support the change.

Remember, if the change is too different from the culture, it will create disconnects and be a continuing stumbling block for successful implementation. If the change is too different from the culture, employees will not believe their leaders and will expect the effort to fail. The result will be that they will not want to invest themselves in something they believe will fail. The change intervention designers need to lay the groundwork before introducing the change effort.

Frameworks, static lists or diagrams of things to remember, can serve as a checklist as you design the implementation plan. The frameworks with which you're most likely familiar include Weisbord's Six-Box Model and McKinsey's Seven-S Framework.

Theories, strategies, models, and approaches all play an important part in change management—even if they do not provide the practical how-to that most of us practitioners need. They provide the underpinnings of the practical change efforts we all implement. You won't use all of them at once, but you should know they exist and are available to help you understand why you might choose to do one thing over another.

History of Change Design

Lewin first presented his Three-Step Change Model in 1947: unfreezing, changing, and refreezing (see table 3-2). Over the years, the second category was changed to transformation and movement. As you can see in table 3-2, this model maintained its integrity, through several iterations, with each "authority" tweaking the model and assigning a different name to the three steps over the years. It wasn't until Kotter published an article in the *Harvard Business Review* in 1995 that focused on his Eight-Step Model that organizational development's change perspective was altered beyond Lewin's three steps. It's been said that the "sign of a good model is one that lasts the test of time . . . and the test of many bright people." That certainly is the case with Lewin's model.

So what do some of these models look like? Well it is interesting to note that Kotter seems to have picked up where Lewin left off. Now many models are takeoffs of Kotter's Eight-Step Model.

Table 3-2. History of Change Models

Year	Model Developer	Change Model
1947	Kurt Lewin	Unfreezing, changing, and refreezing
1977	Richard Beckhard and R. Harris	Present, transition, and future states
1980	Michael Beer	Dissatisfaction x process x model
1983	Rosabeth Moss Kanter	Departures from tradition and crises; strategic decisions and prime movers; and action vehicles and institutionalization
1986	Noel Tichy and Maryanne Devanna	Act I: Awakening; Act II: Mobilizing; and Act III: Epilogue, Reinforcing
1989	David Nadler and Michael Tushman	Energizing, envisioning, enabling
1995	John Kotter	Eight-step model

The six-step CHANGE Model presented in this book builds on these earlier models. This model follows a logical progression of these six steps to create positive, effective, and enduring C-H-A-N-G-E:

Challenge the current state (Step 1).

Harmonize and align leadership (Step 2).

Activate commitment (Step 3).

Nurture and formalize a design (Step 4).

Guide implementation (Step 5).

Evaluate and institutionalize the change (Step 6).

Table 3-3 compares the CHANGE Model with Lewin's model, Kotter's model, David Ulrich's model, and Jeff Evans and Chuck Schaefer's 10 tasks. You can see that the elegant simplicity of Lewin's model has been the basis for the evolution of most change models—the concept of moving from the current state to a preferred future state.

In table 3-3, each model is aligned horizontally to match as closely as possible the steps of this book's CHANGE Model. This allows you to compare the content of each step more easily. As noted, Lewin's model is the most basic and the oldest. Many would argue that his model is no longer appropriate because few organizations can manage to "refreeze." Organizations of today must be agile and flexible. But keep an open mind. Lewin was a true OD pioneer, and most of the current models are based on his simple yet elegant three-step model.

Little was published or changed until Kotter published his model in 1995. His model is built on work that was previously published by Rosabeth Moss

Table 3-3. Comparison of Change Models

CHANGE Model	Lewin's Model	Kotter's Eight-Step Model	Ulrich's Seven-Step Model	Evans and Schaefer's 10 Tasks
Challenge the current state	Unfreeze	1. Establish a sense of urgency	1. Lead change	1. Appreciate the situation
Harmonize and align leadership		2. Create the guiding coalition 3. Develop a vision and strategy	2. Create a shared need 3. Shape a vision	2. Develop strategic alignment 3. Evoke change leadership
Activate commitment	Movement (transformation)	4. Communicate the change vision	4. Mobilize commitment	4. Expand understanding and commitment 5. Analyze processes
Nurture and formalize a design		5. Empower broad-based action	5. Change systems and structures	6. Design process, work, and boundaries 7. Plan implementation 8. Establish metrics
Guide implementation	Refreeze	6. Generate short-term wins	6. Monitor progress	9. Manage transitions
Evaluate and institutionalize the change		7. Consolidate gains and produce more change 8. Anchor new approaches in the culture	7. Make change last	10. Continuous learning and improvement

Sources: Kurt Lewin, "Frontiers in Group Dynamics," *Human Relations* 1 (1951): 5–41; John P. Kotter, *Leading Change* (Boston: Harvard Business School Press, 1996); David Ulrich, *Human Resource Champions* (Boston: Harvard Business School Press, 1998); Jeff Evans and Chuck Schaefer, *Ten Tasks of Change: Demystifying Changing Organizations* (San Francisco: Jossey-Bass/Pfeiffer, 2001).

Winning Idea:
Read the article in which John Kotter first published his concepts. You will find "Leading Change" in the March–April 1995 issue of the *Harvard Business Review.*

Kanter and Kotter's analysis of dozens of change initiatives over the prior 15 years. Though it is highly touted as a superior model, it is academic in nature, providing few realistic suggestions about how to "empower broad-based action" or "how to generate short-term wins." Even so, Kotter's book on the model, *Leading Change,* is excellent reading. Others such as Dan Cohen, have introduced useful, implementable ideas based on the eight steps. David Ulrich's model adds more practicality and reduces the eight steps down to seven. Evans and Schaefer have written a very practical book that includes the 10 tasks they believe are important for effective change management. Although they do not call their work a "model," it is as worthy as most others that have been published. I've added it here because it will be very useful to you.

Each of these models follows a similar path, and all of them require some of the same actions. It is important to recognize that the CHANGE Model follows the same pattern as other well-used models, providing practical exercises and how-tos to support the six steps.

Ethical Considerations

One of the trends shaping the workplace learning and performance profession cited in the ASTD 2004 Competency Study is a "higher ethical bar." Organizational leaders are paying more attention to organizational ethics, including the behaviors required when implementing a change effort. Accepting the responsibility—whether from the perspective of a leader, change agent, or even external consultant—to act in the best interest of the organization and its workforce is so fundamental that we may not even think about it.

Organizational codes of ethics and professional codes of conduct provide frameworks to help you determine what is important to consider. You may have your own code of ethics, but it is important to note that ethical statements are not meant to be an individual statement but rather a collective declaration. If your organization professes a code of ethics, revisit it before beginning an organizational change initiative. Remind all leaders and change agents involved what the organization stands for.

Winning Idea:

To expand your knowledge of this topic, read "Ethics for Trainers," ASTD *Infoline* 250406.

If your organization does not have a code of ethics, you may want to encourage its leaders to discuss the ethical standards they wish to uphold during the change effort. Later, you may use them as a basis for more permanent ethical standards. Here are some ethical considerations as they relate to implementing change. The list is only a start. What is important to you, the organization, and society?

As a change agent, what ethical responsibility do you have to *the organization and the workforce*?

- Honor promises of confidentiality; ensure confidentiality limits are understood by all.
- Raise issues that the organization cannot raise itself.
- Conduct change efforts and other activities honestly and responsibly.
- Introduce new perspectives for consideration.
- Communicate honestly and openly.
- Listen to opposing views.
- Encourage and enable participation.

What ethical responsibility do you have to *the profession and society*?

- Use politics in a positive way, "enlightened politics" as advocated by Peter Block.
- Maintain professional competence.
- Contribute to the profession and the development of other professionals.
- Accept responsibility for and be sensitive to consequences that may alter the lives of others.
- Respect the cultural differences of others.

Winning Idea:

Most professional associations—such as ASTD, the Institute of Management Consultants, and the Academy of Professional Consultants and Advisors—have codes of ethics. If you do not know what your association's code is, call its customer service line and ask that it be sent to you.

What ethical responsibility do you have to *yourself*?

- Be authentic.
- Act with integrity.
- Recognize when self-interest or personal values clash with other responsibilities and seek a positive resolution.
- Continue to learn and grow.
- Address personal needs and shortcoming.

The ethics that guide you and the organization may incorporate other responsibilities. If no ethical statement exists, consider opening the discussion with your organization's leaders.

Overview of the CHANGE Model

The six chapters that follow present a CHANGE Model, with each chapter featuring one of the six steps displayed in figure 3-2.

The CHANGE Model consists of six steps. Each step requires completing distinct and specific tasks, yet as in all models there is also some overlap among the steps. Change is rarely as nice, neat, and linear a process as is presented in this model. Of course, change is led by people and is conducted by people; and people must ultimately change for an organization to change. It is this aspect of "people" that makes change not only exciting but also unpredictable.

The CHANGE Model provides a process that can be used to facilitate an organization through a change effort. Change comes in many formats: developmental change, transformational change, and opportunistic change. Change may be large or small. The CHANGE Model is generic and may be used with any type of change intervention including structural, process, cultural, mergers and acquisitions, growth, downsizing, cost cutting, and others. Each step presents tools and techniques that will help you hone your skills as a change agent or change leader.

Figure 3-2. CHANGE Model

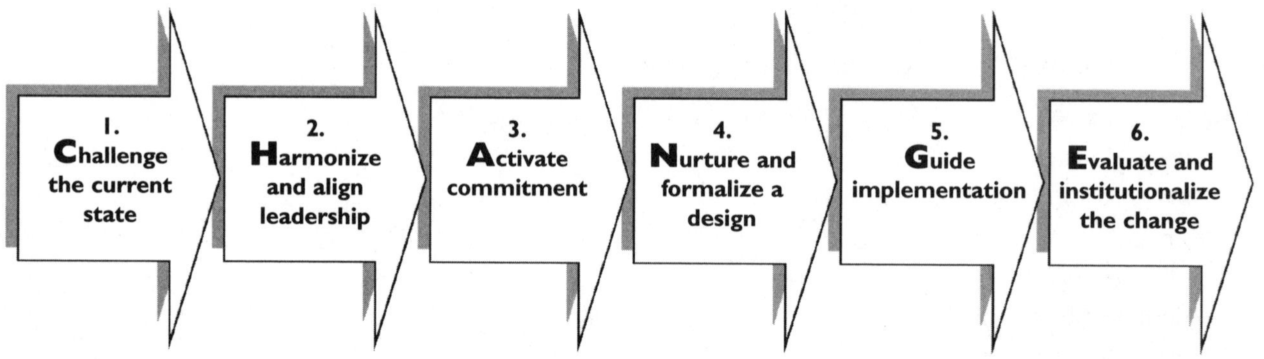

Step 1: Challenge the current state. This step addresses the recognition that something can be different—a preferred future that dares the status quo to innovate. This step is usually initiated by someone at or near the top of the organization who identifies a need for change. It may be externally generated, such as an impending industry regulation or a customer demand. It may be internally generated, such as a high percentage of retirement-eligible personnel on the horizon. Or it may be precipitated by technology upgrades or a merger. This step addresses the question of "why?"

Step 2: Harmonize and align leadership. The first two steps of the CHANGE Model address Lewin's "unfreezing" concept, ensuring that the organization begins the process of unlearning its current habits. Included in the unlearning process in Step 2 is aligning the organization's leadership to understand the organizational need and to identify a way to focus on the challenge from a systems perspective. It is also the leaders' responsibility to begin to model and communicate a consistent message to the rest of the organization about what will happen and the reason it is happening. This step addresses the question of "what?"

Step 3: Activate commitment. As the planning phase moves into the design phase, teams are formed to begin the design, considering what to maintain, what to change, how to get employee buy-in and involvement, and a host of other events to ensure that everything has been considered before implementation begins. The leaders continue to build a strong united front, ensuring commitment to the initiative. The facilitators of change may be required to learn or invent new tools and techniques to develop the implementation plan that helps everyone understand how the change will occur. This step answers the question of "how?"

Step 4: Nurture and formalize a design. Many organizations skip the first three steps and begin their change effort at this point. They decide that a change must take place and then begin to create it. They find, however, that stumbling blocks begin to spring up in their path to prevent the desired change. This step encourages change agents to use tools to formalize the design: conduct a risk assessment, select appropriate metrics, and utilize a number of implementation tools.

Step 5: Guide implementation. This step is *the* action step. The organization is busy keeping the implementation process moving forward. The organization will begin to see some short-term gains, an important result because it provides proof that what was intended with the effort is beginning to bear fruit. Using short-term gains as a springboard, the organization will want to identify ways to increase motivation to accelerate implementation.

Step 6: Evaluate and institutionalize the change. Once implementation has been completed, many organizations are off to find other dragons to slay.

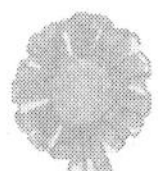

Winning Idea:

Subscribe to an online ethics newsletter. *Ethics Today Online* (www.ethics.org) is a monthly forum for exploring a broad range of organizational ethics and character development issues. The Society for Business Ethics is an international organization engaged in the study of business ethics; see its newsletter at www.societyforbusinessethics.org. Both newsletters are free.

It is essential to encourage people and the organization to accept the desired change and to permanently institutionalize the variations in processes, different products or services, new philosophy, and whatever else was intended to be changed. This step embeds the change in the organizational culture and transforms it into the new reality—the way it is. This step also encourages the organization to prepare for continuous change.

These six steps could be presented in a circle to show the continuous process of change. Imagine the six steps in a spiral, always moving the organization one level higher to an improved level of performance.

How long does this six-step process take? It depends. Is the process merely changing job descriptions or completely changing how the job is done? Does the change deal with how we hire people, or whether we should send the work offshore? In one instance, we helped an organization implement an entire human capital system in just over a year. The effort could have lasted longer, but the crisis of a large number of people retiring in the near future added a natural sense of urgency.

In another case, a company required a change in how it conducted business to move into the European market. Its change leaders estimated two years for implementation, and they spent over nine months in just the first two steps of this model. Many organizations spend no time in planning. This is a big mistake. We know of another example where it took four years to implement a telecommuting plan. Why? Resistance from the middle of the organization stonewalled the plan.

Turn to the next chapter to learn more about Step 1 of the CHANGE Model: Challenge the current state. The CHANGE Model is designed to plan the work and work the plan.

Part II

The Six Steps of CHANGE

Chapter 4

Challenge the Current State (Step 1)

In all things, you must consider the end.
—John Adams

I skate to where the puck is going to be.
—Wayne Gretzky

In This Chapter:

- Collecting and analyzing data
- Assessing organizational readiness for change
- Change management roles
- Creating a compelling business case
- Two considerations for successful change management

Chapter 3 presented an overview of the six-step CHANGE Model. Let's examine the model in more detail, beginning with the first step, "Challenge the current state." This step is both a cerebral step and an action step. A successful change requires thoughtful deliberation and preplanning—whether the perception of the need for the change arose from a strategic planning event, a response to external events, the insertion of new technology, a strain on budgets, a merger or acquisition, or a job restructuring. This chapter addresses this aspect of change with discussions about data collection and organizational readiness.

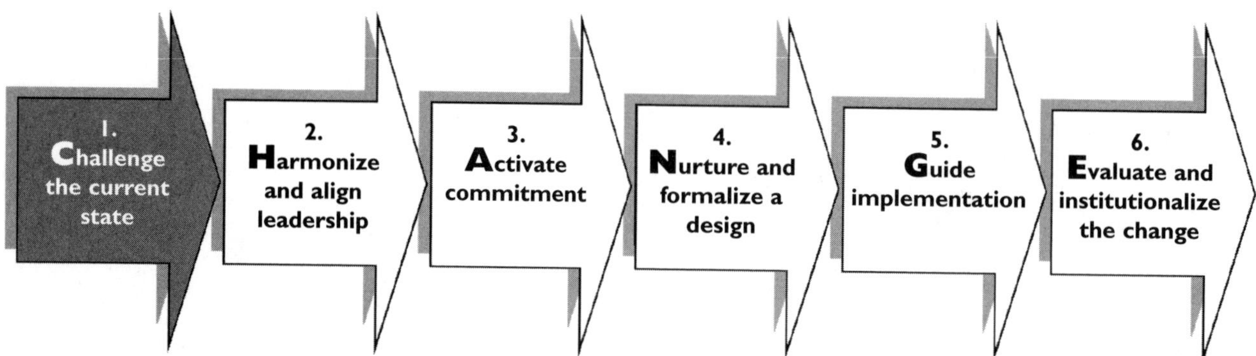

This step is also a call to action, which is addressed in this chapter with discussions about the roles for managing the change as well as building the business case. The business case is the rationale for the change. This step answers the question, "Why?" Why is change necessary? Why is a challenge to the current state required? Four important actions occur in this step that support the "why."

The first action is to collect and analyze data. The work of data gathering and analysis may be completed by the change agent / facilitator or the change leader. At other times, organizations will establish teams to complete this work. When a team collects the data, it becomes an early symbol to the rest of the organization that there is a need to challenge the status quo.

The second action is to determine organizational readiness. Analyzing the organization's readiness for change helps those involved know what they are getting themselves into before it's too late. This preparatory step is often overlooked. Because it requires, in part, an examination of past change implementation efforts, it may be dismissed as unimportant. It may not appear to be the "real" work of getting the change started.

The third action is to establish change management roles. Various roles are established early to shepherd a change initiative from start to finish. These roles ensure that the effort accomplishes what it set out to do. Although the roles may have different designations from organization to organization, the individuals still complete similar tasks to accomplish the change; they lead, champion, sponsor, support, design, plan, and facilitate the change effort.

The fourth action is to build the business case. A business case is a tool that supports planning and decision making about future organizational choices. A business case is built upon the collected data and may require the development of new information that goes beyond existing budgets and business plans. It usually requires assumptions, arbitrary judgments, and the common sense of someone who understands the current situation and can visualize the future potential.

Let's examine each of these four actions in more detail.

Collecting Data

Whether the upcoming change effort is huge, such as a merger or reorganization, or smaller, such as the formation of a new department or job restructuring, the data that you gather becomes the focal point of the change effort. It is the basis on which the change management team makes decisions, the evidence that change is required, the indicator for what should be different, and, in the end, the gauge of success.

Data collection is an ongoing process during any change effort. It is not an end in itself. Though presented during the first step, it will continue to be a part of every step in the process. The type of data collected and how it is analyzed will be dependent upon the information required to design the change effort, the time available to gather data, the organization's readiness for change (we'll say more about this later in the chapter), the scope of the change effort, and the complexity of the change effort.

Why do you need data? William Bridges, the author of *Managing Transitions*, writes, "Stability through change demands clarity about who you are and what you are trying to do." The continuous change era of today's world requires that you are crystal clear about what you are trying to accomplish. Data can help to

- provide content for or clarify the vision for the future state
- identify lessons learned from past change efforts (both internal and external) that could make this effort easier and more effective
- determine the level of support the effort will have and from where
- clarify who will be affected by the change and how much
- estimate the resources required for a successful effort
- assess the strategic gap between where the organization is now and where it wants to be
- identify success rates of other organizations making similar changes
- uncover threats and opportunities.

How do you go about gathering the data? Data collection may be handled by an individual or a team, or in some cases several teams. Data may come from employees, managers, customers, or even existing data files. You may use dozens of methods to gather data, including interviews, focus groups, surveys and questionnaires, observation, existing data reviews, SWOT analysis, and external sources. Let's look briefly at each.

Interviews. You may interview individuals who can provide insight and information about the need for change, lessons learned, cautions, or examples. The advantage to this type of interview is that you can obtain others' ideas about how to handle the situation. A secondary benefit is that you may get early commitment because people have provided input in shaping the design. The downside is that it is time and labor intensive. By the way, although it isn't ideal, interviews may be conducted by telephone as well.

Focus groups. Another approach is a focus group. Somewhat like the interview, you identify key people who can provide information. However, instead of interviewing them individually, you interview them in groups. There are two advantages to this method. First, you can interview more people in a shorter period of time. Second, the members of the focus group piggy-back off each others' ideas. The disadvantage to this approach is that a quiet person may not give his or her point of view and information is skewed by the outspoken members of the group.

Surveys and questionnaires. This approach is used when you want to collect specific information from a large group or a widely dispersed group.

Winning Idea:
If you are a small company, or have limited resources, use online services to gather feedback using surveys. Check out the websites for online survey services, such as www.zoomerang.com and www.monkeysurvey.com. Their processes will save you time and money.

The advantages are that you can include many people and the results are clear cut. The disadvantage is that questionnaires may not allow for free expression or unanticipated information; therefore, you may miss some critical data points. You can resolve this by asking for open-ended comments at the end. Thus, designing a questionnaire includes these steps:

- Use short, simple, direct questions.
- Use language that is correct for the responder.
- Avoid vague words, such as "several" or "most."
- Avoid jargon, abbreviations, and slang.
- Test the questions with an impartial person for biased, leading, or emotional questions.
- Use "other," "don't know," or "not applicable" for the choices for closed-ended questions.
- Ensure that all instructions are clear.
- Ask easy, nonthreatening questions first.
- Group similarly formatted questions together.
- Group related questions together.
- Test pilot the questionnaire for clarity and to ensure that it measures what you intend it to measure.

Observation. This technique works well to learn about people and processes. It is a good technique to use when you expect there will be a need to change behavior or a process (for example, the introduction of a new customer service method, process discrepancies between merging organizations, specific new procedures for welding an I-beam). The most important advantages to this technique is that it provides a realistic view of the situation. In addition, its flexibility allows the observer to detect additional factors that might be important. Observation is a subjective, labor-intensive measure. Because it is not always practical or accurate, it is usually combined with other data collection methods.

Existing data reviews. This technique examines policies and procedures, guidance, sales and profits, safety statistics, turnover, absentee rates, employee demographics, promotion rates, grievances, structural changes, current process flowcharts, and other internal historical records that are currently available and are related to the anticipated change. Review current performance and improvement records, such as balanced scorecard data and Lean Six Sigma reports. Be sure to consider past data collections, such as employee surveys and exit interview data.

Winning Idea:

Your data will only be as good as the questions you create. You will probably want to test a new questionnaire on a small group of people to determine what works and what doesn't. Sometimes questions are misinterpreted. Sometimes questions ask for things they never intended. And sometimes typos prevent good data.

SWOT analysis. SWOT is an acronym for strengths, weaknesses, opportunities, and threats (see figure 4-1). These categories of information are traditional bases of information used in strategic planning. Just as you would do a SWOT analysis during a strategic planning session, it is also important when you are gathering data to determine a change strategy. You must be very deliberate in figuring out what can go wrong as well as what can go right. This tool can help you identify the unintended consequences of your change plan.

External data sources. Gathering data from and about other organizations can provide information about best practices or lessons learned. You may wish to benchmark other organizations through a literature review or an onsite visit.

What criteria will be used to select a data-gathering method? Many factors will determine which method you use. In fact, you will most likely use a combination of the tools listed. Most important is to determine the content required. You will also want to consider these criteria:

- Time: What is your turnaround time?
- Cost: How much money is available? Hiring someone from the outside to conduct focus groups can be costly.
- Comfort level and trust: What is the climate within your organization? Can you rely on the data?

Figure 4-1. SWOT Analysis

	Positives	**Downsides**
Internal	Strengths	Weaknesses
External	Opportunities	Threats

- Size of the population to be surveyed: How many people will need to be asked the questions?
- Confidentiality required: Is confidentiality an issue for individuals in the organization?
- Reliability, validity needed: To what extent is this critical? How will the methodology affect reliability and validity?
- Culture of the organization: What have employees been used to in the past? How will a change in methods be perceived?
- Location of those to be surveyed: Are a large number of people located remotely?

Analyzing Data

Once the data has been gathered, you will most likely want to display the data in charts, graphs, and other visuals to produce a "picture" of why change is important, such as the pie chart in figure 4-2. This will also become a part of your business case. You may wish to separate the data into related segments. One way to do this is to divide the data into three groups: findings, options and opportunities, and recommendations.

Findings include all the data points, both subjective and objective, that you identify. Generally, a list of these begins long before an organization decides to initiate a change effort. These facts are often the impetus for the change. Findings include the verifiable information, statistics, and evidence in the form of both quantifiable and qualifiable data that creates the change story. It may be presented as a bulleted list.

Options and opportunities are the conclusions drawn from the findings. As you can imagine, the list becomes shorter as you glean pertinent options and combine opportunities into fewer steps. This can be presented as a list of options and alternatives, as pros and cons of maintaining the status quo, or as a list of conclusions stating the relevant evidence, such as "Based on our findings, an opportunity exists to . . ."

Figure 4-2. Data Point Graphic Example

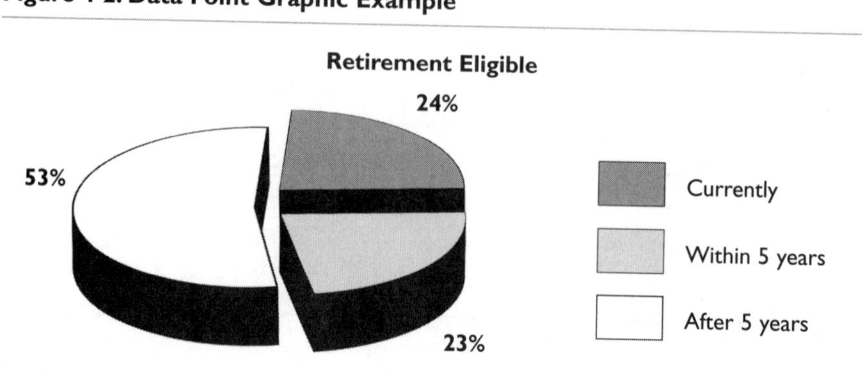

Recommendations are the result of your analysis. Here again, you may present them in several ways. They may be in the form of alternatives that need further research, a leadership decision, or additional resources. Recommendations will generally flow logically from the statements of findings and of options and opportunities.

The data collected will be used in many ways. It will most likely provide the statistics and the information for the business case; create a springboard for the assumptions; present the impetus for a risk assessment; form the basis for the change management team's decisions; constitute the evidence that change is required; and, in the end, serve as the measure of success. Your data should tell a story to support the change effort.

Winning Idea:

Be sure that you have identified the root causes of problems and are not basing your conclusions on symptoms. Use the Five-Why Technique to identify the root cause, which you will find as activity 1 in chapter 11.

Assessing Organizational Readiness for Change

Determining an organization's propensity for change is one of the most important aspects of the first step in the CHANGE Model. There is often a desire to omit this step because it relies on reviewing the organization's past history and experiences with change. The historical perspective sets the stage for what to expect and provides direction for what needs to occur for success. Two tools are presented here to help you determine your organization's readiness for a change intervention:

- organizational change readiness audit
- change readiness predictor.

Both these tools will help you understand your organization's readiness. Neither will give you a definitive "go/no-go" decision, but they will

- create valuable discussion among leaders and employees
- alert you to the areas that may pose problems during the implementation
- create awareness throughout the organization, depending upon how widely the tools are used
- identify preliminary actions that may be required before a change initiative launch.

Conducting an organizational change readiness audit is much like being a reporter. You will interview individuals in your organization seeking answers to the questions of who, what, when, how, and why. Be sure to select a wide variety of people, interviewing a diagonal slice throughout the organization that covers executives, managers, supervisors, the front line, and support people. Include as many departments as possible, seeking out both employees who are new and those who have been around a long time, and both those who are positive and those who are less than positive. Ask about organization-wide change and department-wide change, change efforts that were successful and those that were not, simple change and complex efforts.

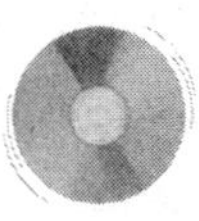

The questions in worksheet 4-1 can serve as a guide to get you started (an image of this worksheet is given here, and the reader can find a full-size version in appendix D and a PDF version on the companion CD-ROM). They address both past change experiences and what can be expected in the current culture. Consider tailoring the questions to meet your organization's needs. The organizational change readiness audit provides subjective conclusions.

The change readiness predictor, shown in worksheet 4-2, provides more objective results (full-size versions available in appendix D and companion CD-ROM). Use this checklist with a group of key managers and change facilitators. A comparison of the scores will generate a useful discussion. The facilitator can direct the discussion toward how to ensure success. If scores are unusually low, the group can explore the reasons for the low scores and determine what preliminary actions need to be taken to increase chances for success. For example, if unions or other constraints pose a situation that may prevent success, identify what it will take to eliminate or reduce the constraint. If management support is rated low, identify what it will take to increase management support. See activity 2 in chapter 11 for a process and suggested discussion questions.

Understanding organizational readiness is critical when planning for change. An organization's change effort has a higher chance of success when

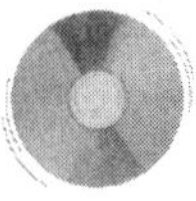

Worksheet 4-1. Organizational Change Readiness Audit

Past change efforts and results:

- In what past change effort have you been involved?
- What do you remember about each change effort:
  - —What happened? Why?
  - —When did this occur?
  - —What were the results?
- How could the change efforts of the past been more successful?
- What would you have done differently?
- What lessons were learned from past change efforts?

Current readiness for change:

- How would you describe the current culture and its readiness to make a change?
- What change efforts are you aware of that are occurring now? Please describe them:
  - —What specifically is happening?
  - —Why is the change occurring?
  - —Is there anything special about the timing?
  - —Who is responsible for the change?
  - —How would you describe employees' willingness to change?
- What barriers exist that will prevent change from occurring, e.g., lack of resources, lack of leadership, dysfunctional culture, rewarded for the wrong thing, policies, procedures, labor agreements, access to the workforce?
- How quickly do employees adjust to changes? Why?
- What must occur for the anticipated change effort to succeed?
- Who should lead the anticipated change effort? Why?
- Who should be involved in this change effort?
- What is the best time to initiate this change?
- What metrics shall we use to measure results?
- What resources are required?
- How would you like to be involved?
- How will we know we have been successful?
- What is the best way to celebrate success?
- What should I have asked, but didn't?

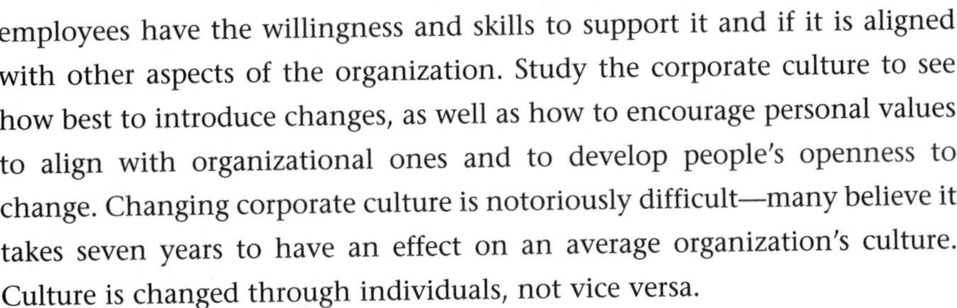

Worksheet 4-2. Change Readiness Predictor

Indicate the degree to which each of the dimensions is a concern to you with regard to your organization's change readiness. Circle the number under the appropriate heading for each factor. Dimensions have been scaled according to their relative importance in predicting the receptivity to change. Total the scores for an overall change readiness index.

	Degree of Concern				
Dimension	**No**	**Little**	**Moderate**	**Substantial**	**Critical**
Comprehensive variables:					
Size of change	4	3	2	1	0
Current internal stress	4	3	2	1	0
External impact	4	3	2	1	0
Change history	4	3	2	1	0
Supportive culture	4	3	2	1	0
Clear internal processes	4	3	2	1	0
Resources:					
Access to workforce	8	6	4	2	0
Workforce flexibility/agility	8	6	4	2	0
Unions/other constraints	8	6	4	2	0
Time commitment	8	6	4	2	0
Money available	8	6	4	2	0
Employee considerations:					
Workforce talent	12	9	6	3	0
Executive leadership	12	9	6	3	0
Skilled change agents	12	9	6	3	0
Management support	12	9	6	3	0
Total the scores for all dimensions:					

Total all columns: ______

If the total change readiness score is: less than 50, conduct crisis intervention before beginning; if it is between 50 and 69, proceed with caution, taking all steps in the process to ensure success; if it is greater than 69, the organization is ready for the planned change.

Source: ebb associates inc, 2004.

employees have the willingness and skills to support it and if it is aligned with other aspects of the organization. Study the corporate culture to see how best to introduce changes, as well as how to encourage personal values to align with organizational ones and to develop people's openness to change. Changing corporate culture is notoriously difficult—many believe it takes seven years to have an effect on an average organization's culture. Culture is changed through individuals, not vice versa.

Change Management Roles

A variety of roles ensures that a change initiative accomplishes its intentions. The main roles include those of change leader, change agent, and change management team.

Change leader. A change leader, sometimes called a champion or a sponsor, is the person who legitimizes the change. The leader's (or sponsor's or champion's) role may appear different in different organizations depending upon the level of involvement and the separation of roles. In some cases, the leader, champion, sponsor, and change agent will all be the same person. The next chapter delves into the role of the leader.

When reading about the business case, you may have gotten the impression that if the rationale for change is compelling enough, if the business case musters arguments that are logical and persuasive, there is little for the leader to do. Nothing could be further from the truth. A few visits to the podium to tell the preferred story of the future will not win the hearts, hands, and minds of employees. The change leader must be involved from start to finish. Due to the leader's constant involvement, each of the subsequent chapters adds more to this role.

Change agent. A change agent, sometimes called a change facilitator (both terms are used in this book), may have the most difficult role (see table 4-1). The change agent may conduct the change as the leader's key implementation person, making decisions when the leader is unavailable. Or the change agent may serve as the support person with little decision-making authority, but ensuring that deadlines are met and tasks completed. This person may not be in the forefront, but he or she ensures that everything is taken care of behind the scenes, guaranteeing that the effort runs as smoothly as possible.

What do you notice as you examine table 4-1? If you look closely, you can see that effective change agents must embody opposite qualities:

- They must be collaborative yet have the ability to influence.
- They must be tolerant of ambiguity yet persistent.
- They must think realistically and logically yet be creative.
- They must have a big picture vision yet be detail oriented.
- They must be both process oriented and people oriented.

This book has been written especially for the change agent/facilitator who must have multiple skills and must be able to work under various kinds of pressure, handling diverse responsibilities, all with diplomatic aplomb. Activity 3 in chapter 11 creates an opportunity for you and other change agents to discuss these characteristics.

Change management team. The planning and design in most efforts is the work of the change management team, sometimes referred to as the transi-

Table 4-1. Characteristics of an Effective Change Agent/Facilitator

• Credible	• Process oriented	• Creative idea person
• Trusted and respected	• Customer focused	• Collaborator
• Tolerant of ambiguity	• Organizational knowledge	• Achievement oriented
• Self-confident	• Big picture vision	• Realistic
• Persistent	• Detail orientation	• Sense of timing
• Ability to influence	• People person	• Interest in change
• Attentive listener	• Passion	• Logical thinker
• Eager for improvement	• Deals well with negativity	• Excellent communicator

tion team or the implementation team. The next chapter offers advice for establishing a change management team. Although the team is typically not selected until the next step, you will want to begin thinking about who might fill that role.

Creating a Compelling Business Case

Winning Idea:
In *The Heart of Change Field Guide,* Dan Cohen presents a comprehensive change readiness assessment. You will find it in his last chapter.

You will use the data you have gathered to create the business case for the change. Your organization may have another name, such as the "value proposition" or "the compelling story." A business case uses the data that have been gathered and creates a preferred future scenario. In addition to the data that you want to highlight, a business case may also include benchmarking competitors or industry leaders; a vision of the preferred future and/or mission; results of an employee survey, interviews, or focus groups; financial data; Lean Six Sigma data; impact statements; or other support that adds to the compelling nature of the case for change. It will tell the story. In most for-profit organizations, the business case will have a financial justification providing an adequate return-on-investment.

A business case presents the rationale for change, using a logical flow of scope, evidence, and analysis that leads up to the recommendations. Like a legal case prepared for a court presentation, both the attorney and the business case developer have the flexibility to select or ignore evidence, formulate arguments, and develop the final presentation. In both cases, their abilities to tell a convincing story with compelling facts and logical narrative will determine the effectiveness of the outcome. And like a jury in a court, the employees will make the decision about whether they were convinced.

There are many ways to structure a business case. Even so, certain fundamentals must provide the underlying foundation for a solid, "winning" business case. For example, a good business case presents all the pros and cons, all the costs and benefits. A good business case presents *all* the relevant facts but *only* those relevant to the case. It is not cluttered with interesting but unrelated content. A good business case presents a logical and informative story and should help create a sense of urgency.

A business case template is presented as worksheet 4-3 (full-size versions of this worksheet available in appendix D and on CD-ROM). However, as you build your case, remember that, like a trial attorney, you will find no single right way to develop the case. You may need more or less information in your case. It will depend on the complexities of your case and your "jury."

Creating a compelling business case creates a dialog that is different from the one that typically occurs in an organization. It may present data that leaders have been ignoring, introduce ideas that many have not considered,

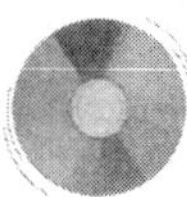

Worksheet 4-3. Business Case Template

Remember: A business case should include what is necessary to include—no more, no less. This template may be more (or less) than what you need for an initial business case presentation.

I. Cover Page

Include the change name, date, version if appropriate.

II. Executive Summary

Provide a concise summary of the key highlights. Although located at the front of the document, it is written last. It should be no more than two pages that stand alone as a single source of the overall project purpose, goals, proposed actions, cost/benefits, risks, and success criteria.

III. Current Situation

Present an introduction to the business case analysis to:

A. Provide rationale/purpose of the business case
B. Identify the sponsor
C. Describe the problem or opportunity
D. Describe the current situation
E. Include relevant data and analysis of the options.

IV. Project Description

Provide the objective, a clear definition of what the change will accomplish. Explain how the change will address the business problem/opportunity identified in III. Include:

A. Measurable goals and objectives (ensuring they support the business needs)
B. Performance measures that will be used to determine outcomes
C. Assumptions and how they were arrived
D. Proposed new environment
E. Major effort milestone dates.

V. Environmental Analysis and Alternatives

Describe pertinent current events outside the organization, discuss what other organizations have done, and propose viable options.

VI. Business and Operational Impact

Identify the impact for each stakeholder and technology assessment.

A. Business impact such as a change in service or products provided, or focus or direction of a department
B. Operational impact such as staff training required or reduction of resources
C. Technology requirements.

VII. Preliminary Risk Assessment

Optional at the early stages of a change effort, but if included it identifies the potential risks, assesses risk for impact and probability, and presents a mitigation plan for each risk.

VIII. Cost/Benefit Analysis

Evaluate the costs and benefits associated with each viable alternative.

Worksheet 4-3. Business Case Template (continued)

IX. Implementation Timeline and Strategy

Define the scope of the effort that may include:

A. Project management controls
B. Analysis, development, and design
C. Transitions and training
D. Resources required and from where.

X. Conclusion and Final Recommendations

Provide a selected alternative based on an overall evaluation in terms of impact, risk, and cost/benefit. Next steps are also usually included.

or tell a story of an impending future—good or bad. Whatever the story, a business case is one way to help create a sense of urgency. Be sure that the business case is strong enough to attract two audiences:

- senior-level management
- all the affected employees.

Why a sense of urgency? We all become comfortable with the way things are. Unfortunately, comfort can lead to complacency. And complacency is the enemy of change. Complacency may occur for many reasons: ample current resources, a limited knowledge of competitors, denial due to past success, a shoot-the-messenger culture, the lack of an obvious crisis, inaccurate or inappropriate metrics, and a host of other situations that insulate leaders and the workforce from reality.

In the book *Leading Change*, John P. Kotter identifies other ways to increase urgency:

- Communication suggestions, such as disclosing more of the organization's problems and concerns in newsletters and through management communication
- Surprising suggestions, such as eliminating symbols of executive privilege and excess
- Practical suggestions, such as insisting that more people be held accountable for broader performance measures
- Realistic suggestions, such as sharing more negative customer satisfaction and financial performance data with more people
- Uncomfortable suggestions, such as insisting that employees speak with dissatisfied customers, disgruntled shareholders, and discouraged suppliers.

Discussions of global competition or loss of market share can sometimes create a sense of urgency. Honest customer feedback may create a sense of urgency. Sometimes the sense of urgency comes naturally from the outside, such as an energy crisis or seminal events like recent health care errors. As a consultant, I am frequently hired to deliver the bad news, to expose relevant data, or to force discussions about failures in the organization. Any of these might work. The key in most change efforts is that the workforce needs to have a compelling reason, a sense of urgency, and it needs to be led by committed executives.

Two Considerations for Successful Change Management

A final, but important thought: A successful change management effort requires planning for and integrating both the people affected by the change and the process selected to implement the change. The change journey will not meet organizational objectives if an effective process is not implemented. However, keep in mind that it is the employees, the people, who will implement that process. Both employees and processes usually must change.

I have identified several reasons why you must be focused throughout the change effort on both components. However, a good practical exercise to complete as you conclude this first step is to identify more reasons why it is critical for a change agent to consider both aspects of change: the people requirements and the implementation process. Add your thoughts to the lists in table 4-2.

Table 4-2. Considerations for Change

Consider People Requirements:	Consider the Implementation Process:
• People must implement the plan • Emotions contribute to success • People need to know what's in it for them • Resistance can prevent success • People make it happen	• It keeps everyone focused • A proven model leads to proven results • It prevents chaos • You must consider its impact on the customer • It provides a foundation

Checklist for Step 1: Challenge the Current State

- ❑ Data is available to define the required change.
- ❑ Data and information have been gathered and analyzed.
- ❑ The organizational readiness has been evaluated, weak areas have been identified, and a plan is in place where necessary to safeguard against the lack of readiness.
- ❑ Change management roles have been clearly defined.
- ❑ Change management roles have been assigned: change leader, change champion, change agent / facilitator, implementation team.
- ❑ A business case has been created to verify and rationalize the change on the basis of relevant data.
- ❑ The leaders of the change effort appreciate that a successful effort requires planning for both the change process as well as the people who are affected by the change.

Chapter 5

Harmonize and Align Leadership (Step 2)

It is not because things are difficult that we do not dare, it is because we do not dare that things are difficult.
—Seneca

In This Chapter:

- A change leader's VIEW for success
- A successful change leader's day
- Strategies for change leaders
- Selecting and building a change implementation team
- Developing an aligned team
- Creating a vision
- Designing communication plans

One of the key triumphs of a change effort is bringing leadership together to speak as one, with one message, one voice, and one purpose. Major change is difficult to accomplish without a central organizational force behind it in the form of unified leadership and a cohesive team to implement the various aspects of the change initiative.

It goes without saying that the change effort should be aligned with the organization's strategic plan. The strategic plan guides the direction. The leaders should focus on results, not activities. What is the organization trying to accomplish with the initiative?

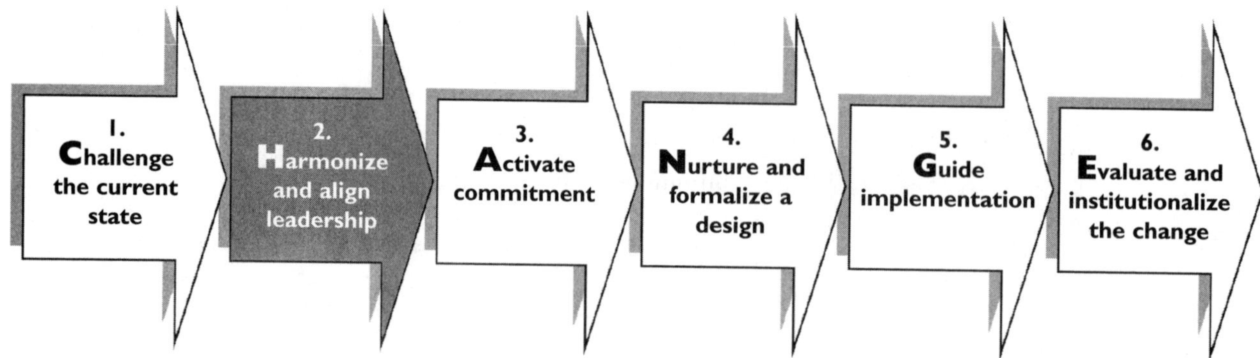

An aligned leadership goes a long way to ensuring success. Despite our best intentions, change efforts do not usually proceed as planned. David Nadler, the author of *Champions of Change*, said it best, "The truth is that change is inherently messy. It is always complicated. It invariably involves a massive array of sharply conflicting demands. Despite the best-laid plans, things never happen in exactly the right order. . . . Most important, the reality of change in the organizational trenches defies rigid academic models as well as superficial management fads."

What does this mean? Change may take longer than you anticipate. It may not go the way you planned. It requires strong leadership. There is no one right way. The fact is, you must be prepared for anything. Having an aligned leadership that is behind a compelling vision supported by a strong implementation team is a change leader's dream. This chapter addresses these efforts. It also provides a template and ideas for informing the rest of the organization with communication plans.

Step 2 in the CHANGE Model can be considered the "what" step. What is the intent of the change? What is the vision? What needs to be done? What does leadership need to do? What do we tell everyone?

A Change Leader's VIEW for Success

To succeed, a change leader needs a V-I-E-W that is

Visionary

Inspiring

Enthusiastic

Wise.

A successful leader of change has many characteristics that bring about a successful result. Most important is the VIEW the leader takes of change. An effective leader views change enthusiastically and is concerned with the entire organization and its workforce. The leader is someone who can establish a direction for a distant future, taking into account the entire organizational structure and how changes in one area will affect other areas. The leader of change will inspire the members of the workforce to follow where they wouldn't dare to go alone. The successful leader is visionary, inspiring, enthusiastic, and wise. It is useful to list the characteristics of each aspect:

Visionary:

- Ability to imagine the future; focuses on results
- Articulate
- Strategic thinker, risk taker
- Challenges the status quo.

Inspiring:

- Sells the vision, benefits, and what can be
- Genuine; models the change intended
- Passionate; evokes followers to get on board
- Engaging; builds alliances across the organization
- Trusts others, and is trusted.

Enthusiastic:

- Energizes others to overcome barriers
- Involves others; is collaborative
- Open to others' ideas; allows for mistakes
- Rewards and appreciates others.

Wise:

- Has wisdom in many areas
- Knowledgeable about organizations, politics, people, and processes
- Analytical; understands data and can develop solutions
- Anticipates and addresses issues
- Exudes business acumen
- Is a problem solver.

A Successful Change Leader's Day

How would leaders VIEW change appropriately? How would successful leaders of change spend a typical day? What behaviors would you see leaders doing in each of the four areas?

Visionary. Visionary leaders articulate the vision for change—what the organization will be like. They create scenarios for employees, painting a picture that others can understand. They are big picture thinkers and may frustrate some employees by not having all the details figured out. Although they map out a general strategy to give the vision life, they trust that other team members will take care of the details to make it happen. They are comfortable with the ambiguity of the process. They are living the vision as if it had already been realized, and thereby modeling what is expected and challenging those who are not on board. You may find them looking out windows more often than looking down halls.

Inspiring. Inspiring leaders sell the vision and its benefits. They talk with conviction and are committed to bringing others along. They get the work done through teams, both vertically and horizontally. The messages they communicate are consistent and exciting yet tailored for each particular audience. They are excellent spontaneous speakers, thinking quickly and easily integrating fragments of the change process. Motivating people comes natural to them, and they are aware of how their behavior affects others. They are trusted by and trusting of others. You will most often find them in a small group caught up in a passionate discussion of almost any topic.

Enthusiastic. When leaders are enthusiastic, they look for the best in everything. They encourage others to connect and celebrate. They are good at turning failure into a positive learning opportunity, and they like working in teams. They are truly interested in others, remembering and using individuals' names. They like to use the appreciative inquiry process and are forgiving when others make mistakes. Although they are open to others' ideas, they also are persistent about overcoming roadblocks, and they do not take detours easily. You will most often find them collaborating with others on projects and recognition opportunities.

Wise. Wise leaders exude confidence. They are savvy in the way that they balance a vision with data. They are competent and credible, managing crises with aplomb. They think before they speak, ensuring that they have a logical response. People come to them to solve problems and address challenges. They are good at connecting the dots from one project or issue to another. They are usually organized and efficient. They are politically astute and well networked, which ensures that they know how to obtain resources. They like a friendly debate, listening carefully to what others say, using the information at a later time. You will find them asking questions in many situations, especially "Why?" and "How?"

Strategies for Change Leaders

Change challenges us all, but no more so than the leaders of organizations that are experiencing change. Leading change is not for the faint of heart. Leaders must have a plan for change without knowing all the ramifications. They must be prepared for the unexpected with answers. They must take the heat when things go wrong and share the glory when things go right. They must remain positive when they continue to receive negative news. And they must do all of this with diplomacy and grace. How can a leader be prepared for all this?

Barriers That Prevent Change

Facilitating organizational change is rarely easy. Barriers pop up where you least expect them. Preventing barriers from occurring with good planning is the best strategy. (In chapter 11, you will find activities 6 and 7 on the topic of barriers, which you may wish to use with your change team as preparation and team awareness exercises.) Here is a list of the most common barriers:

- lack of clear vision
- insufficient information
- limited management support
- lack of communication
- organizational complacency
- lack of change leadership experience
- lack of planning for resistance
- lack of time
- insufficient resources allocated
- policies not aligned to the change
- poor follow-through
- lack of rewards for change or consequences for not changing.

As you can see, most of these should not occur if planning is done well. A change agent can use this list as a discussion starter with the leader.

Advice for the Change Leader

If you are the change agent, you may find yourself coaching the leader of your change effort. It is an excellent role; your leader needs an extra pair of ears and eyes, as well as some commonsense advice. These may seem sensible to you, but all leaders need to be reminded of what they already know. If you are the leader of change and reading this book, tap into these suggestions to move the change along more rapidly and with fewer glitches.

Provide information about the change early and often. You simply cannot overcommunicate. Change cannot be communicated in a single meeting. No matter how often you say it, it won't be often enough. Some won't hear it; some won't understand it. In some cases, if the change is very different, it may be impossible for people to comprehend because it is so far outside the boundaries for what they "know" is the correct answer. How can you prevent this from happening? Speak to the needs of the person with whom you are talking rather than repeating the same "change story" over and over. Identify the concern that each person or group will have, and tell the story from their perspective. What do the members of the group think they are sacrificing for the change? What do they believe is their insurmountable hurdle? Help them identify their personal roadblocks and find a way through them. What is the reward from their perspective?

Seek input from employees. Ask for information. Ask "How's it going?" Ask for ideas. Ask for suggestions. Ask for help. Ask how they like the new plans. Ask in person. Ask in an email. Ask in a presentation. The key is asking for input and then listening—really listening to their responses and replying thoughtfully. Remember, communicating begins with listening.

Celebrate resistance. Too often, people resist silently. When someone is willing to resist aloud, celebrate! Appreciate that someone was willing to take a risk to tell the emperor he's not dressed for the occasion. When someone shares honest reasons for not joining the parade, listen carefully without judging the message, without shooting the messenger. What can you learn?

Communicate the preferred future vision. You may get tired of telling the same story and painting the same future vision. Your employees will not. Be sure to incorporate actions and events as the vision begins to become a reality. Sometimes employees just need practical ideas that can be implemented realistically.

Ask if you are moving too fast. You need buy-in from the key people who have a stake in the outcome. Many change efforts have failed due to a lack of support. If some group is not on board, slow down. Remember, you have most likely been intimately involved with this preferred future longer than anyone else. Allow them time to catch up with you.

Be careful of what you promise. All of us have heard numerous timeworn statements that are so common they become a part of our everyday conversation. However, they take on a new (and not always good) meaning when they come from leaders without a full explanation. How many of the following promises have you heard?

- We've got the right people on this.
- There won't be any layoffs.
- I have no hidden agenda.
- This will be the last time . . .
- The customer will appreciate this . . .
- It will not have an impact on bonuses.
- This will save you time.
- We'll see results in less than 90 days.

Be honest about the reasons for change; acknowledge potential losses. Honesty, honesty, honesty. Enough said.

Explain what will not change, as well as what will change. Too often, leaders get wrapped up in all that is changing and forget to remind others of all that is going to stay the same. People need to hear what will not change. This becomes a security blanket to many.

Model the behavior you expect. Few employees believe what they hear or read. They believe what they see. All eyes are on you. Do you model what you expect others to do as it relates to the ensuing change? If you want to change people's behavior, model what you expect to see from others.

Admit fears, concerns, and unknowns. What concerns you the most about the change? Admitting your concerns and that you do not have all the answers makes you appear human. Be careful here, however. You need to exude confidence that the effort will progress successfully and that the right answer will be available when necessary. If you do not address the unknowns or major concerns, employees will think you are avoiding the discussion (which you probably are!). Avoiding difficult discussions undermines your credibility and the integrity of the effort.

Be sure to share the WIIFM (what's in it for me) aspect. A business case can tell a compelling story about why the organization will benefit. As the leader, you need to spend equal time telling employees what's in it for them. Every employee will be at a different place along the change continuum. Some may be in the early stages of awareness, others may have the desire to make anticipated changes but not yet have acquired the skills, and still others may be ready to act but not be on board with the direction. Once you recognize the stage a person is at, it is easier for you to deliver a message that is truly personalized.

Prepare the system for change. Be sure that enough resources are in place to cover all the peripheral systems that will be affected by the change. Have you considered how increasing the number of sales in one department will affect the workload in the shipping department? Or the service technicians available to support the additional number of customers? Or the increased number of transactions in accounts receivable? When you change one thing, it affects everything else in the system.

Provide the training, coaching, and tools that employees need. If you want people to change, you must give them the skills and knowledge they need to support the change. Be sure it is just in time, practical, and adds value.

Selecting and Building a Change Implementation Team

A change implementation team should be selected early to initiate the change. In large organizations, people may work full time on the team during the transition. The more significant, complex, and time-consuming the proposed change, the more important it is that time and people be dedicated to the change effort—whether full or part time.

Who should be on this team? John Kotter advises managers to "put together a group with enough power to lead the change and get them to work together like a team." Remember the team members must model the preferred culture—act as living symbols of the new organization. Establishing the implementation team and getting it to work together is one of the key tasks of the change agent and leader.

A study conducted by the Corporate Leadership Council examined change management teams in various industries. The profiled companies reported a significant number of competencies that are required of change team members. Those mentioned most often included business experience, effective communication and presentation skills, people skills, analytical thinking, project management, and process design. There are probably no surprises in the results.

Winning Idea:
If your organization does not yet belong to the Corporate Leadership Council, check them out at www.corporateleadershipcouncil.com. They conduct research, provide white papers for members, offer professional networking, and have a wealth of knowledge.

What is more important may be the ability to select team members who have qualities that will ensure results. As you are establishing the team, keep it to a manageable size. It will depend on the size of your organization. You need to strive for a balance between a team that includes members from all the important employment groups and a team that is small and agile enough to make quick decisions. As you select team members, consider these characteristics. Remember, you want to form a team that has balanced representation, is respected, and has the right attitude. The team selection activity (activity 8) in chapter 11 may help. To sum up, here are lists of the main aspects of a productive team.

Select the right people:

- position power and key players
- informal leaders
- expertise
- credibility
- leadership and management skills
- respected and trusted.

Select people from the right areas:

- diagonal cross-section of the organization
- represents all stakeholders
- good representation from the most critical area.

Select people with the right attitude:

- positive
- trusting
- problem solvers
- enthusiastic
- persistent.

The Team's Role

The change implementation team provides guidance for the change effort. It defines the strategies, sanctions the process, and provides needed resources—both people and dollars. It usually has been given formal authority, although the most successful teams include one or two members of the executive suite. Success is dependent upon the executive team being a part of the change and not delegating the responsibility down. If this team is at a very high level (as for a large organization-wide effort), it may have subteams that address tasks such as further analysis, design, and the details of planning. Begin to clarify the team's role at its first meeting (see figure 5-1).

People Who Should Not Be on the Team

To be efficient, there are some people you may wish to avoid putting on the team. You know what a bother it is to deal with those who have unusual ideas, are negative, or are braggers. Yet don't be too fast to eliminate some

Figure 5-1. Sample Agenda for First Team Meeting

Agenda for First Team Meeting
[Date]

Objectives:

- To clarify the intent of the charter
- To define ground rules as a team
- To explore next steps

9:00 Welcome and Introductions

9:10 Background

9:20 Goals for Today

9:25 Our Mission: Review Charter

9:40 Roles and Responsibilities:
Team Lead, Facilitator, and Team Members

9:45 Future Meeting Location, Day, and Time
Ground Rules
- Decision making
- Attendance
- Promptness
- Participation
- Conversational courtesies
- Assignments
- Routine chores
- Agendas, minutes, records
- Other

10:15 Review Actions and Evaluate Meeting
Questions and Discussion

10:30 Adjourn

of those whom you judge to be troublemakers. Someone with off-the-wall ideas may stimulate creative thinking during difficult problem solving. Sometimes people are negative because it is the only way they think they can be heard. If you listen carefully, they may have good ideas that have been ignored too often. A braggart may have never received appropriate recognition.

I once was approached by a senior executive who was apologizing in advance for placing Margaret on a team that I would facilitate. He stated that although she had the most knowledge and the most to gain from the team's success, he was concerned that she would create problems on the team. According to him, she was negative, lacked people skills, and was an all around "bully." She started out as the manager described, but as the team addressed ground rules, lived up to expectations, and became successful, Margaret turned around. She contributed, stepped in for the leader, and transferred the skills she learned on the team to the workplace. Margaret is a true success story.

I am not telling you to add one troublemaker to every team. I am saying that you may want to reconsider an individual's reputation and determine if the person might play an important role on the implementation teams. Be cautious. Make wise decisions as you establish your teams.

Developing an Aligned Team

As the change facilitator, you can't do it alone. So take time in selecting and building a change implementation team to help you champion the change effort. Use this checklist to ensure that you have aligned the team to the change effort:

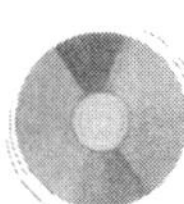

- ✓ Ensure that the charter clearly defines the purpose, boundaries, and the role of the team (for a sample charter, see worksheet 5-1; full-size versions available in appendix D and on CD-ROM).
- ✓ Encourage frank discussion at all meetings; position should not be a barrier to anyone's open and candid comments.
- ✓ Invite the change leader (CEO, president, director) to attend the first meeting to clearly define the vision and to answer questions or allay concerns.
- ✓ Ensure that the team members demonstrate commitment through involvement; they should not simply make decisions and pass the "work" on to someone on their staff.
- ✓ Build strong relationships among the members by building trust through open communication and a healthy approach to conflict.
- ✓ Make decisions by consensus as much as possible.

Worksheet 5-1. Sample Team Charter

Team: Talent Resourcing Team Charter

Team Lead: Dr. Frank Carr

Purpose: Address the following Human Capital Strategy Team recommendations:

- Ensure that all team results/recommendations match the greater organizational Human Capital Strategy requirements.
- Align recruitment strategies with workforce planning efforts to close critical position gaps and to employ a diverse workforce.
- Modify the internal recruitment process to eliminate gaps caused by late initiation of the hiring process.
- Educate the organization's leadership about HR flexibilities.
- Develop a succession planning process that
  - —holds leaders accountable
  - —identifies 25 to 50 key positions requiring a succession plans
  - —identifies governance and management responsibilities
  - —creates developmental opportunities that prepare employees to compete for key positions.
- Integrate diversity into the overall recruitment and succession plans.

Anticipated deliverables and products:

- Plan and timeline to modify the recruitment process.
- Set of options for increasing diversity in the recruitment and succession plans.
- Define and initiate the succession planning process.
- Communication plan to inform leadership.

Findings from Strategy Team:

- Organization lacks workforce planning and processes.
- Forty-six percent of the current workforce can retire in the next five years.
- The average age of the workforce is 49.29 (up from 48.75 in three years).
- Workforce is not representative of the nation's diversity.
- Processes related to recruitment and hiring are cumbersome and time consuming
- There is very little turnover. Most managers believe the hiring process takes too long and would like more help in identifying and marketing to a more diverse set of prospective candidates.
- Nearly 90 percent of organizations worldwide reported that succession management was a top corporate priority this past year.
- Over half of the organizations interviewed implement a Corporate Management Development Program focusing on formal training for managers including succession planning.

Conclusions:

- Organization's ability to identify workforce imbalances is inadequate.
- National pipelines of talent are shrinking.
- Duplication and a lack of connection exist among the many education and recruitment programs within our offices and our sister organizations.
- Coordinated and integrated recruiting programs and career development with cross-cutting career paths will benefit the enterprise.
- Branding career opportunities for the enterprise could position it as "employer of choice" and increase the enterprise's ability to compete for high talent.

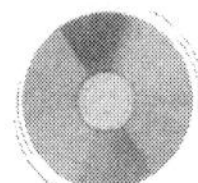

Worksheet 5-1. Sample Team Charter (continued)

Team competencies required:

- Basic understanding of the hiring process
- Experience with the recruitment and hiring process
- Understands the critical need for a succession planning process
- Respected leaders (formal and informal)
- Excellent communication skills
- Inspires high team performance
- Creative, innovative, risk taker
- Viewed as a progressive thought leader
- Results oriented, strategic thinker
- Analytical skills
- Positive attitude.

Team members:

Scott Blacks (finance)
Maggie Masters (HR)
John Connally (contracts)
Leila Ramirez (global)
Tom Paluszkiewicz (research)
Preston Grant (S&T)
Janet Johnshoy (legal)

Guidance:

- Meet at least biweekly for 3–4 hours.
- Preliminary report due on November 7.
- Team Leader Progress Meetings will be held biweekly.
- Final implementation plan due on December 7.
- Obtain commitment from Human Resources, Contracts, and Finance.
- Facilitation will be provided by ebb associates.

______________________________ CEO   __________ Date

- ✓ Address all difficult issues head on as soon as you suspect there may be self-interest issues, hidden agendas, or political plays.
- ✓ As a team, explore the change vision and whether it is aligned with the current corporate vision and direction; have the team make system changes to create the alignment.
- ✓ Clearly define the performance measures for the team—for example, milestones, decisions to be made, resources to be dedicated, and other accountabilities—and hold team members accountable.
- ✓ Identify ways that the team interfaces with other stakeholders, teams, and departments.
- ✓ If energy wanes, hold a rejuvenation offsite; this team must be the epitome of support, dedication, and commitment to maintain a sense of urgency.
- ✓ Keep the decision-making process moving forward.
- ✓ Find ways for the team members to inspire people outside the team.
- ✓ Schedule the change leader to attend meetings to participate in decisions, to provide information, and to voice confidence in the team.

Remember, select the right people—those who are credible with upper management, those who are respected by employees at all levels of the organization, and those who are capable of obtaining the necessary resources to accomplish the task. Ensure that the team members are from the right areas. Be sure that you have engaged representatives from areas that will be most affected by the change. Be sure that you have individuals on the team who have access to the data and/or resources you will need to accomplish your mission. And be sure that you have a diverse group that will provide a wide range of perspectives and disciplines to make good decisions.

Winning Idea:

Hand out copies of the book *Our Iceberg Is Melting* to members of the implementation team. Discuss the book at one of the earlier meetings. Use the questions in the back of the book to initiate discussion. The most powerful message is sent when the change leader is a part of the discussion—or even leads it. Later you may wish to buy books for other employees of the company—especially if the implementation team starts speaking in "penguin"!

Although you are selecting people who are from a diagonal cross section of the organization, you need people who are not parochial but who can think corporately. Also select those who have the right attitude. Select those who are positive and persistent even when facing roadblocks—those with a "git 'er done" attitude. Once you have selected the team, you can get them involved in helping to create the vision.

Creating a Vision

"A vision is something that lives within people, not a few words on a piece of paper," state Jeff Evans and Chuck Schaefer, the authors of *Ten Tasks of Change*. A vision paints the picture of the preferred future. It creates urgency and draws people in. It focuses on the end state. If you have a vision of the future, you can create it. Sure, you may possibly bumble and stumble your way into a positive outcome, but a vision will get you to the right destination much faster.

A vision puts aside present problems and describes the preferred future. Employees who have a vision guiding the direction of the change have a reason to take action to make change a reality. Employees need to see and understand the future if you want them to move toward it. They need a target at which to aim. People tend to be more supportive and willing to help create something that they understand.

The vision may be a part of the business case (see Step 1), or it may be created at this point. The vision is short and lends support to the business case. A vision for change helps to explain

- what the organization needs
- why the organization needs what it does.

An effective vision should be

- *Exciting, yet feasible.* The vision should create passion in the members of the workforce, yet they should be able to see that it is practical, realistic, and attainable.
- *Global, yet personal.* The vision must be a unifying statement, yet it must be compellingly meaningful to every individual.
- *Focused, yet flexible.* That is, it should be specific enough to delineate the direction, yet general enough to accommodate individual initiative and adjustment to changing conditions.
- *Practical, yet optimistic.* A vision is candid about necessary sacrifices, but it also creates a commitment to a better future.

Visions live in people, not on the paper on which they are written. They appeal to the heart as well as the brain. The vision must offer employees something better than they currently have.

Create a Vision Statement

Unless your change was born of a crisis, you'll need to create a vision of the preferred future. When a crisis is the impetus for the change, the results may write the vision of the future—preferred or not. Kotter in *Leading Change* tells us that there is no one way to create a vision and that "vision creation is almost always a messy, difficult, and sometimes emotionally charged exercise." It is usually an iterative process that flows back and forth between individuals and groups. Here's a simplified process that works.

Bring the senior management team and the team that gathered the data for the change effort together. Have them discuss what the vision needs to accomplish. You may wish to stimulate discussion with some pre-reading. Have the data and the recommendations available.

Next, have the individuals write words and phrases on pages that are taped to a wall. Out of these words, have each person begin to craft a vision statement. Read each aloud and post the statements. As a group, narrow it down as much as you can. Ensure that everyone is participating in the discussion. Get as close to final copy as you can. Ask for a couple of volunteers to finalize the wordsmithing. Have them bring it back to the group for further discussion and agreement at another meeting.

The most effective visions I've seen were

- written by managers and leaders—not by their communications departments or an outside consultant (you must have the buy-in of a shared common vision—one with some sweat equity in it)
- short and to the point—not long and detailed
- authentic and direct—not necessarily polished and refined
- written using words that are meaningful to the organization—as opposed to a sample of fine prose.

Creative Vision Creation

Do you want to be more creative when creating the vision? We know one organization that hired an artist to attend all their change strategy meetings. In the end, he created a picture of their vision for change. They had a large poster hung in the entrance to their building and even had smaller versions printed on paper placemats for the corporate cafeteria. They thought a vision should be visual!

Your organization's vision for change should paint a picture of the preferred future. Though it may seem an arduous task, creating the vision is actually the easiest step of the visioning process. You still need to ensure that it is clearly communicated, that you are building commitment to the vision, and that what people do is aligned to the vision.

Winning Idea:

Hire a consultant from a company like Grove Consulting International (www.grove.com). An artist will observe and capture the ideas that arise from your early planning meetings and will create a 4-by-8-foot visual that you can use to discuss the future of the organization. You may even want to post it in a common area where people can add comments with Post-it notes.

Your vision may be just a sentence long, or it may be a story or two. Or like the vision of the organization mentioned above, it may be a picture. The following ideas may spark a creative visioning session for your organization. Consider these ideas to describe your future. They may just be idea starters, or they may actually turn into the vision:

- Create an award for your organization due to a successful change effort
- Present a brief skit
- Write and sing a song
- Write a radio commercial
- Prepare the CEO's to-do list for 10 years out
- Write a TV newscast
- Create a podcast
- Write a short story
- Write a poem
- Create a metaphor

- Choreograph a dance
- Draw a picture
- Create a poster for a future corporate event
- Develop a jingle
- Create new job titles.

You may select several of these activities to stimulate creativity. Identify similar themes and words that occur as a result and begin writing a vision statement from that point.

Designing Communication Plans

You can never communicate too much during a change initiative. Once you have the data, a business case, and a compelling vision, you can begin to establish a communication plan. You will add to it and change it as you work through the change effort, but you should begin to plan communication now. Update the communication plan as you continue to work through the steps in the CHANGE process.

During a change effort, employees have very similar questions. If you eavesdrop on any discussion, you will hear the same concerns:

- What is happening?
- Why do we need to change now?
- How will it affect me?
- How can I get more information?

Keep these questions in mind as you design the communication plan. You will identify four types of information that need to be incorporated into the communication plan.

Identify people who will need to know and who will want to know. Frequently, you can easily segment the population into logical groups: senior management, branch offices, factory workforce, administrative staff, southeastern region, customers, first-line supervisors, and others. Be sure that you don't take the "who" for granted. It is wiser to communicate beyond the normal boundaries than to forget a segment of the workforce.

Identify the specific information that should be shared. Often, you may begin with a core message and tailor it to various locations and/or departments. It will help to identify the issues that will be most critical to each department and/or location. If rumors start (and they will), dispel them immediately. Sometimes a rumor is so outrageous that you may want to laugh it off, thinking that no one will believe it. Not true. Rumors left to themselves will get out of hand. Be sure that the information you share is consistent, appropriate, and useful to the workforce. Repeat the reason for the organizational change in every message until you are sure that it is clearly understood by at least 75 percent of the workforce.

Identify the methods you have available to you for delivering the information. You will, of course, want to leverage technology, but don't overdue it. The delete button is just too handy. In fact, research shows that employees prefer to receive information from their immediate supervisor; therefore, there is a critical need to keep that group informed. Also, most employees will tell you that they prefer face-to-face meetings to other forms of communication. This is especially true when conveying difficult news.

Identify the timeline for delivering the information. A communication planning grid like the one in worksheet 5-2 is useful to see the layout of the plan (available in appendix D and on CD-ROM). You can readily see

- How often you are communicating with specific groups
- Which topics are being presented and in what sequence
- How heavy or light the message delivery load is for various people
- The types of media that are used in a span of time.

Successful implementation teams anticipate and head off employee responses to difficult aspects of the change. Keep employees updated frequently; some organizations recommend daily. One manager I work with holds daily 15-minute meetings. He calls them "stand ups" because they are short, informative, up-to-the-minute reports on what is changing. Finally, hold people accountable for delivering the message on time every time. A communication plan is useless if it is not implemented.

Communication Plan Tips

Keep these communication plan tips in mind:

- Communicate often; repetition is good.
- Leaders of the change should be available to communicate informally.
- Use a variety of communication methods.
- Keep it simple; use stories, metaphors, and analogies.
- Develop an elevator speech and an escalator speech: The first is a sentence or two; the second adds explanation.
- Share the responsibility of communicating with those on the periphery who would like to be more involved.
- Exchange information "hats" to demonstrate alignment; for example, the finance director can deliver the information about the human resources design.
- Listen; a communication plan needs to be two-way.

Worksheet 5-2. Communication Plan Template

Date	Targeted Audience	Message/Event	Method/Media	Delivery	Status
2/7	Administrative officers	What do performance goals mean to me?	Brown bag lunch	Talent manager	Complete
3/9	All	Why competencies are important to all of us	Podcast	CEO presents; HR designs	Designed and approved; ready for delivery
Monday at 9 a.m. Weekly	Managers	Weekly phone call with leadership for updates	Conference call	Change facilitator/ implementation team	Ongoing
Thursdays, 1:00-3:30	All	Answer questions within department	30-minute listening Posts	Implementation team member	Ongoing

Research shows that managers and direct supervisors are the most effective senders of messages regarding change. Even excellent communicating managers need support and ideas for keeping the message in front of their employees. Consider creating original communication events that are unique and a little out of the ordinary for your company. They will capture attention. Add them to your communication plan.

Methods that have been used successfully include meetings (leadership briefs, all-employee, department huddles, town halls), coaching, newsletters, bulletin board notices, posters, telephone trees, telephone hotlines, podcasts, wikis, blogs, ask-an-expert websites, website messages, training (peer, classroom, CD, videos, Internet-based), "central" change rooms, demonstrations, brown bag lunches, recognition days, electronic suggestion box, survival kits, letters or videos sent home, CD-ROM recordings, booklets, brochures, cheat sheets and job aids, check stuffers, wallet cards, weekly conference calls, employee recognition kits, and one-to-one contact.

The chief naval officer (CNO) was adamant that all his naval officers deliver a consistent message to everyone. He gave a one-page, laminated executive summary to all Navy leaders. The page included the mission, goals, strategic

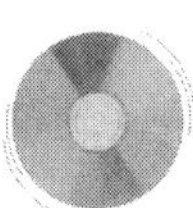

Winning Idea:

Try some of these communication ideas that are distinctive enough to stand out above the rest:

- Success story of the week published on the organization's intranet
- Challenge of the week
- The Friday Five: Five things that must be completed by 5 p.m. on Friday
- Hold milestone parties
- Host a "Coaches Corner" on the intranet to share ideas across the organization
- Post progress on a thermometer or other measure
- Pulse the organization with a wiki
- Post success stories on an "It Works!" board; include testimonials from early adopters
- Memo from top management: "All we know" and "All we don't know!" heads off questions and prevents gossip.

priorities, communication goals, and implementation plans. He wanted to ensure that everyone was "singing from the same sheet of music."

Getting attention. What if you really need to get attention with your message? One of the most creative and useful techniques was tried when senior leadership manned a "Lucy Booth" in the lobby of their building during several lunch hours. They staffed it with executives, and employees could get their questions answered or their complaints heard for a quarter. The proceeds went to charity. Several other ideas that people have shared with me include:

- Initiate a teaser campaign by supplying a couple of clues each week until someone identifies the "mystery" and wins a prize.
- Publish puzzles or wuzzles and award prizes to the winners.
- Kick off the effort with a "feel good" event, such as a jazz band; the CEO could even be a member of the band.
- Have managers dressed as waiters "serving" questions to employees to ask or answer during a corporate meeting.
- Have a couple of hours of speed chatting with upper management—a takeoff from speed dating.
- Use a reality-themed show experience.
- Post a newsletter on bathroom doors for "Potty Training."
- Pitch a tent, and deliver the message around a circus theme complete with cotton candy and popcorn.

What About Emergency Communication?

No matter how well you plan or how perfect and creative your communication plan is, something will go awry. You can be prepared for these emergency situations. One organization I worked with established a process to address the volatile environment in which it operated. When a crisis occurred, a series of questions and answers were created by the communications department at headquarters. With the press of a send button, the message was delivered electronically. Supervisors in a dozen locations throughout the world could download the information and cut it to size to fit in their pockets. Usually no more than five questions and short responses were included in each communication. The supervisor's briefing cards provided just enough information, took no time at all, and were ready in real time so that supervisors always had the answers at their fingertips.

Checklist for Step 2: Harmonize and Align Leadership

- ❑ The change leader's qualifications have been assessed.
- ❑ The leader and change agent have discussed the requirements of an effective change leader.
- ❑ We have identified the right people, from the right areas, with the right attitude for the change implementation team. They are:

  ____

  ____

  ____

  ____

  ____

  ____

  ____

  ____

- ❑ The change implementation team held its first meeting and understands the need to work together as a team.
- ❑ We have reviewed a list of possible barriers that could delay or prevent change and have created counterstrategies for each.
- ❑ The organization has created a compelling vision that is
  - — exciting, yet feasible
  - — global, yet personal
  - — focused, yet flexible
  - — practical, yet optimistic.
- ❑ We have ensured that senior-level change support is highly visible.
- ❑ We have developed a communication plan.

Chapter 6

Activate Commitment (Step 3)

The winners of tomorrow will deal proactively with chaos, will look at the chaos per se as the source of market advantage, not as a problem to be got around.
—Tom Peters

It doesn't work to leap a 20-foot chasm in two 10-foot jumps.
—American proverb

In This Chapter:

- Designing the implementation plan
- Building critical mass
- Understanding and predicting reactions to change
- Buying in: Taking the vision trip from compelling to common

You've developed a fundamental description of the proposed change with a business case. You have created a compelling vision and aligned leadership. Step 3 creates the road map that allows the organization to move forward toward the change. It discusses thoughts on designing an implementation plan. It also addresses one of the biggest stumbling blocks of change implementation: understanding and predicting resistance.

Step 3 is the point where you, and the teams that were established in Step 2, fill in the details of the implementation. You formalize the design that up to

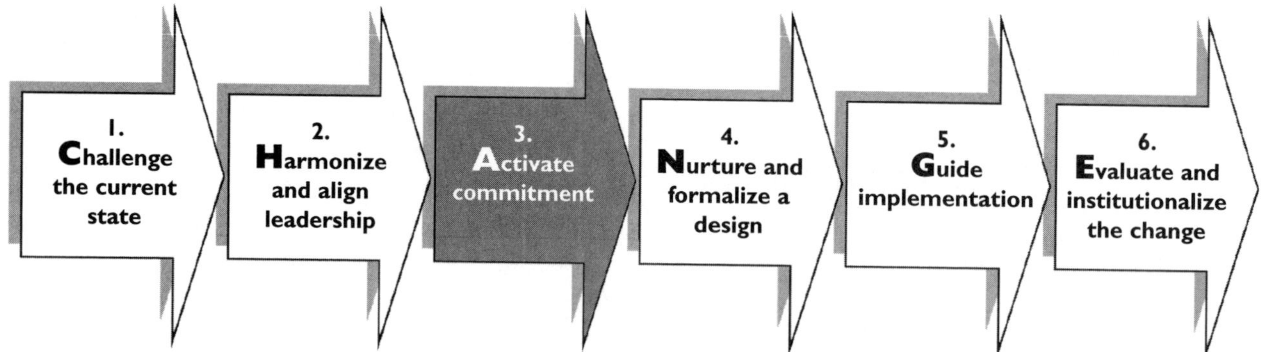

this point has been merely a vision and a business case developed to gain support, obtain input, and generate enthusiasm for the change effort. Until now, you have been addressing the "what" of change. This design step requires that you determine the how of change—how to implement what has been purported to be good for the organization.

This does not mean that those involved in the change effort up to this point have not been focused on how to make the change happen. But it is one thing to say "We can do this" and another to provide the guidance, specific direction, and coordinated instructions to those who are ready and willing to make the change.

Step 3 is like deciding to drive to the other side of the country. You can talk about it for months, tell people about what will be different when you arrive, and paint a clear picture of your vision for what you will do. However, at some point you need to plan how you are going to get there: by what process, what timeline, what route. That is what happens in this step. You will put a plan together to determine the process by which the transformation will occur.

Step 3 is the "how" step. How do we know if we need an implementation plan? How do we design the implementation plan? How do we marshal resources? How do we build a critical mass to ensure the effort moves forward efficiently? How do we predict and address reactions to change? How do we attain buy-in to the vision?

Let's begin by answering the first question: How do we design the implementation plan? And do we even need one?

Designing the Implementation Plan

Is a plan necessary? You bet it is! An article in the October 30, 2000, edition of the *Wall Street Journal* examined high-profile deals that failed. One of the top three reasons cited was inadequate planning. Creating an overall implementation plan before the project starts provides you with these benefits.

Road map. Just as you will need a road map and a plan to follow if you drive to the other side of the country, you need a plan to take you from where you are to the final vision. A road map keeps you from driving around in circles.

Resource estimate. You get an estimate before you build a house to determine the cost and time to complete building. An implementation plan will help you determine the total effort and duration, the kind and number of resources you will need, and how the organization can address these needs.

Communication tool. Informing the organization needs to be done as soon as possible. An implementation plan provides something tangible to deliver early to the members of the workforce. It will answer some of their questions and raise others. It will begin the open dialog among the implementation designers and the rest of the organization.

Systematic organizer. Just as you keep a calendar so that you do not double book events and so that you remember what you need to do when, an implementation plan lays out the who will do what by when. It also presents how various entities will interact, parameters of the change, issues to address, communication and training plans, and a hundred other details. Defining these all up front will help to manage expectations.

Credibility for the effort. An implementation plan documents that thought and planning have occurred. Although the plan will probably not provide all the support you need, it promotes confidence that you have invested time and money and have thought through many of the details.

OK, So We Need an Implementation Plan

You are finally ready to put pen to paper—or marker to pad—to plan the implementation. Of course this is not the first time you and the teams will have thought about and discussed how to generate the change. The "how" is the heart and matter of the effort. Designing the implementation plan is a lot of work and generally comes out of numerous discussions within the implementation team.

Design is intuitive, not entirely logical. It is a creative unfolding of a plan, not necessarily a logical proposition. It is iterative, and it emanates from the people creating the design and implementation teams. Team members have been wallowing in information, data, findings, and statistics. It is now that you will harness their potential to design the implementation plan.

Having said that, remember that you are not dealing with just a single element. An organization is a system. An integrated approach is required because a fundamental change will most likely change all the aspects of the organization. There is no one plan that will work for every implementation, though a variation of an action plan is often a place to start. Many transformational change efforts are so large and distinctive that there is not going to be one right way to design the implementation.

The steps in designing an implementation plan are presented here in several categories. Remember, however, that you may take some or all the steps. Although the list appears to have a logical sequence, you may not do them in the order presented here. You may be doing some in sequence and some in parallel, and even feel as if you are doing all of them at the same time! So here are the steps, category by category, along with questions that arise:

Review current information:

- Review the data gathered in Step 1. Does it tell the correct story? Do you need different data? More data?
- Review the business case. Does it tell the whole story? From a systems perspective?
- Sell the reason for the change. Do people understand what has caused the need for change? Too often, leaders spend most of their time selling the solution when people need to understand the problem.

Create the road map to complete the key steps:

- Ensure that those on the design team understand the intended outcome—the immediate outcome and how this change will affect the organization in the distant future. Where does the organization want to be, and by when?
- State the change goals and a clear description of the end state.
- Identify specific actions required to achieve the goals.
- Identify completion dates for each action.
- Identify and allocate dedicated resources, experts, and consultants.
- Ensure that the level of investment is appropriate for success.
- Assign responsibility and define accountability: Define how stakeholders will be involved with the design, and plan for transitional management. Does leadership understand that the transition will take longer than the change?

Ensure that the plan will be successful:

- Explore and document the impact of each of the actions on other organizational systems.
- Decide whether to conduct a pilot program; if yes, which target population will provide the most useful feedback?
- Do you need to conduct additional benchmarking of other organizations? Did the earlier data gathering address this adequately?
- Enlist people in the organization who have expertise in handling change. What needs to be done to tap into their experience?
- What does each manager need to do to support the change? What support can be provided to each?
- Who are the informal leaders? How can you get them involved?

- Be prepared to adapt the strategy and the steps along the way.
- Manage the endings. Did you plan for the endings? What can you do to help employees deal more successfully with the endings?
- How soon do you initiate a risk assessment plan?
- Establish a monitoring plan and a champion who has an overall view of the implementation. Is the reporting process readily observable to all?
- Establish the accountability. Is it clearly defined? What are the consequences? What are the rewards?

Prepare people for the change:

- Identify all the ways people can be a part of the planning and implementation. How do you ensure that everyone who wants to be involved is involved?
- Depending upon the size of the change, gather data on employee attitudes toward the change.
- Define choices employees have—and yes, leaving is a choice.
- Ensure that opportunities for candid dialog are included in the communication plan.
- Move people out of the timeworn conversations of the past into hopeful communications of the future. What are these conversations? How do you create the setting? What are the conversation starters? How can they motivate each other?
- Address the losses people experience: relationships, security, identity, habits, familiar processes, customary tools. How can the good-byes be orchestrated to be meaningful?
- Identify the preferred behaviors. Which will occur easily? Which will require incentives to happen?
- Provide the necessary training and coaching. Do you know who will need training, and when? How will coaching occur? Will it be requested or assigned?

Refine the communication plan:

- Does the plan sell, inform, and motivate?
- Now that the implementation plan has been refined, does the communication plan still meet the organization's needs? What about the timeline?
- Does the plan ensure communication with those most affected?
- Identify a way to obtain employee feedback.
- Integrate employee feedback. What plans have been made to integrate the feedback into the design? What guidelines are in place to respond to employees?

Winning Idea:

Check out Rick Maurer's website (www.beyondresistance.com), which is jam-packed with over 100 articles, tips, and tools in change categories such as getting started, leading change, keeping change alive, getting back on track, and making a compelling case for change.

Recognize and celebrate success:

- Celebrate in the short term. How will you acknowledge and communicate the small successes?
- Celebrate larger milestones and long-term wins. How will you recognize the larger gains?
- Develop strategies for increasing commitment.

Documentation and Other Tasks

You will "learn as you go." You may find yourself creating something new every day. To initiate the implementation planning, begin with an action plan. An example can be found in table 6-1. Your information technology department can help you set up Microsoft Project or other software that can help you manage and document the plan.

Some of the other types of material you may need to develop to document the implementation include budgets, timelines, plans of action and milestones, crosswalk reports, communication plans, and monitoring and evaluation plans. If you are the change agent, you may be asked to do a number of things you've never done before. Like what? Check out table 6-2.

Building Critical Mass

Although you will never be able to obtain 100 percent commitment to a change effort, it is well worth the effort to determine the minimum amount of commitment required to be successful. One tool that has been around for many years but still serves an important purpose is a stakeholder or commitment chart. The original concept for this chart is credited to Richard Beckhard. This tool helps you to determine what constitutes a critical mass for this particular change intervention. Think about the various players in the organization. Do you need each stakeholder to:

- Make the change occur by leading?
- Help change occur by providing resources?
- Allow change to occur by not blocking progress?

Design a grid, like the one in table 6-3, to help you determine the effort needed to reach the level of commitment required of each key player. For each person, indicate the level of desired commitment (lead the change, provide resources, or allow the change to occur) in the appropriate column with a D (desired). Once you have identified the desired state for all players, revisit the list and locate the present state for each person. Indicate the person's "current commitment" with a C. Draw an arrow from the Cs to the Ds to indicate how much movement is needed. If the C and the D are in the same cell, you already have the desired commitment. If they are not, develop a strategy for getting them to the desired level of commitment. The strategy may include

Table 6-1. Action Plan Example

Action	Decision/Resources	Who	Next Steps	Timeframe
Institute PMP		HR	Note: Ensure that VP stays engaged.	Completed
Reshape workforce		TM	Begin departmental workforce review–data-gathering process; complete analysis prior to strategic planning.	Begin February
Web to consolidate CHART	Funding to develop	HR, IT	Jose to do a sanity check to get other opinions whether this is wise. If yes, HR begin to work with IT.	February
Prompt hiring decisions		HR, TM	HR present data; share with department heads at weekly meeting; continue track data & present. HR could be total solution.	Begin February; present April; review October
Create recruit/hiring toolkit		HR	Begin to design kit and distribute with instructions/training to use.	Begin February
Select diversity coordinator	$180,000	TM	TM begins recruitment; help departments to build department diversity plans.	March
Minority matching funds	$500,000		Greene and Walker are decision makers; identify ideas from all departments; include in budget.	Decision by June
Performance appraisal: discuss diversity		TM, CEO	CEO needs to discuss with department heads and cascade down. Coordinate with NSPS training, *Career Development Handbook.*	Begin March
Build relationships with professional societies		Frank	Frank will present at S&T Leadership meeting; ebb prepare a one-page reference document.	March
Formal/informal succession process		TM, CEO	CEO introduce informal and cascade down; design formal pilot; incorporate with *Career Development Handbook* and competency work; involve department heads.	Begin May; complete July
Identify key positions essential to organization		TM	List positions; confirm with directors.	Completed
Increase use of interdepartmental teams		TM	Will suggest to CEO when appropriate; LSS to ensure this is happening; need lead team that charters opportunities.	
Polish corporate image to recruiting groups	Funding website	HR, PA, IT	HR and PA work together to improve website and other tools.	Plan to implement; due March

Table 6-2. You May be Asked to . . .

• Create the ROI documentation • Revise policies and procedures • Redesign processes • Write new job descriptions • Facilitate a shared vision • Develop white papers • Review plans with individuals • Maintain documents that update progress • Troubleshoot teams with problems • Measure customer satisfaction • Design training plans • Determine how to exchange information • Solve problems of all kinds • Conduct impact studies • Establish a transition process • Identify individuals to complete the work • Plan to move people or departments • Create value propositions • Maintain attendance sheets • Schedule interviews • Identify team members • Establish further design work	• Develop standard operating procedures • Brainstorm solutions • Implement pilots • Develop executives' talking points • Create rationales • Meet with departments, teams, or leaders • Build teams • Identify appropriate metrics • Address employee dissatisfaction • Pair employees for coaching • Create organizational charts • Create a pacing strategy • Determine the critical path • Establish issue-resolution forums • Identify IT requirements • Develop strategies to address resistance • Draft emails for senior management • Roll out timelines • Develop interview questions • Conduct risk assessments • Plan celebrations

Table 6-3. Stakeholder Chart

Stakeholder	No Involvement	Allow Change to Occur	Provide Resources	Lead the Change
1.			CD	
2.			C ——→	D
3.	C ——→	D		
4.		CD		
5.		C ——→	——→	D
6.		D ←——	C	

Key: D = desired; C = current commitment.

Source: Based on a concept by Richard Beckhard and R.T. Harris, *Organization Transitions: Managing Complex Change*, 2nd ed. (Reading, MA: Addison-Wesley, 1987).

problem solving, role modeling, education, responsibility assignment, and political clarification. Note that key player number 6 is not an error. It is possible to have too much commitment—which can get in the way of the plan.

What can leadership do to help build commitment—to move people in the direction required? Set the tone with your own dedication to the effort. It is difficult at times to understand why people are not yet on board with the change. Step back and appreciate how much longer you have been involved mentally in the change. You need to give others a chance to catch up with you. So continue to lead by example, model expectations, practice what you preach, and take an active role in reaching out to those whose commitment you need. A leader's wholehearted involvement as a change leader is critical at this time.

Understanding and Predicting Reactions to Change

Everett Rogers's research categorizes five types of individuals based on their acceptance of change (see figure 6-1):

- *Innovators* make up 2.5 percent and are the first to embrace change. They are adventurous and proud of it.
- *Early adopters* make up 13.5 percent of the population and like to take on new challenges. They are trend setters who stay informed and are generally influential members of organizations.
- *The early majority*, 34 percent of all individuals, are thoughtful about change initially and become positive based on observation. They become deliberate acceptors of the change.
- *The late majority* includes the 34 percent of the population who are skeptical about change. They may change due to peer pressure.
- *Laggards* include 16 percent of all individuals who hold onto the past and resist change. This becomes a problem if they reject the change completely. Someone in a workshop once said, "Oh! Those are the CAVE dwellers—Colleagues Against Virtually Everything!"

Resisting Change

Turn to figure 6-2 and read the message in the Spiral of Change (also available on CD-ROM). Do not read further until you complete the message.

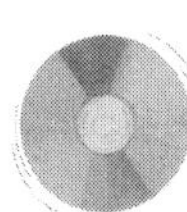

Once you have completed (or given up) reading the Spiral of Change, think about these questions:

- How did you feel when you started this exercise?
- How did it change overtime?
- Why did that happen?
- If you gave up and quit, why?
- If you made it to the end, was it worth the effort? Why?

Figure 6-1. Change Acceptance

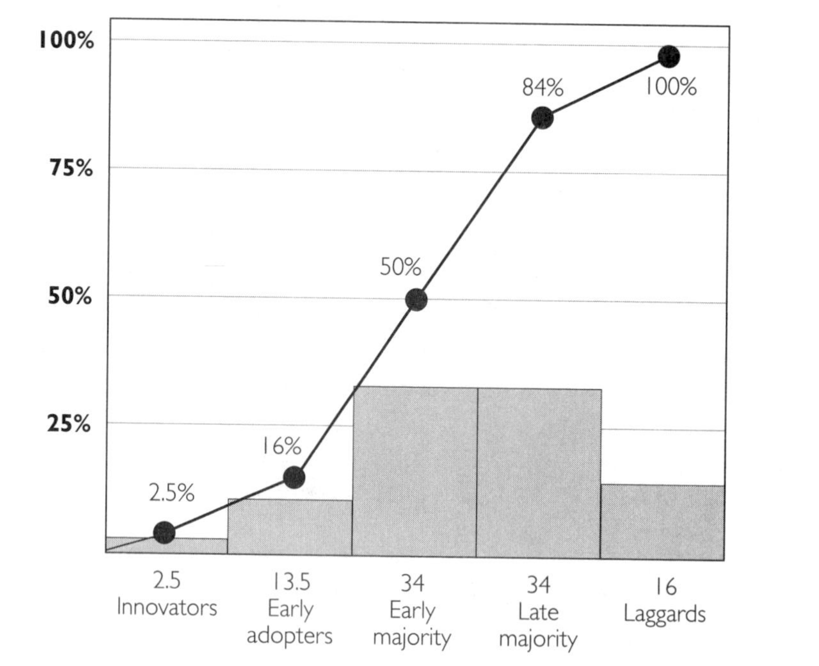

Source: Based on Everett M. Rogers, *Diffusion of Innovations,* 4th ed. (New York: Free Press, 1995).

Figure 6-2. Spiral of Change

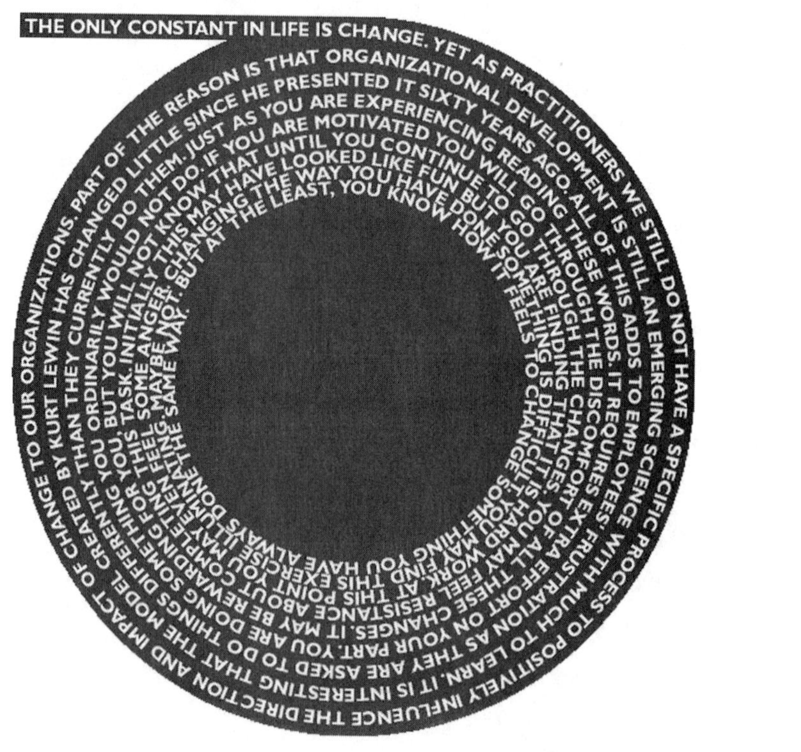

Source: ebb associates inc.

What you have just experienced is resistance to change, albeit a small amount. You probably felt excited when you started the exercise and became bored or maybe even irritated as the message continued on and on. If you reached the end, you probably were a bit disappointed because the end does not reveal anything very exciting except that you have completed the task. Some of you perhaps gave up and quit because you thought you had better ways to spend your time. And throughout the experience, you could see no good reason how reading in a spiral was any better than the "way you've always done it before," left to right! (You can find this exercise in activity 9 in chapter 11.)

Your feelings during the Spiral of Change replicate on a small scale those feelings employees experience when organizations implement change. What can you do? Read on to the next paragraphs.

When conducting a change management workshop, I almost always move participants' seating arrangements, ensuring that everyone is at a different table and with different participants. When I ask how it feels to sit in a different seat, the responses include "Uncomfortable," "Sitting in the same seat is habitual," "It's irritating," "Don't like someone messing with my routine." Negative responses occur even though everyone is in the workshop to learn more about how to manage change.

When I ask "What would have made the change more acceptable?" the responses include "An early warning," "Being a part of the design," "Being able to select my own location," or "Asking for my preferences." Although the exercise creates discomfort, it is one of the best experiential learning activities I know.

Whether resistance manifests itself as foot dragging or foot stomping, you can anticipate that you'll experience at least some. Why do so many employees find change to be uncomfortable and unwanted? Is all change resisted? No, of course not. Is it that people just want an early warning? Want to be a part of the design? Perhaps. Let's look at four thought leaders' perspectives of resistance.

Rick Maurer, the author of *Beyond the Wall of Resistance*, believes that you can identify resistance at three levels and then treat it appropriately.

Level 1 is based on information and may come from

- lack of information
- disagreement with the idea itself
- lack of exposure
- confusion.

Level 2 is physiological and emotional and may come from fear of a perceived

- loss of power or control
- loss of status or respect

- feeling of too much to do
- feeling of incompetence.

Level 3 may come from

- a personal history of mistrust
- cultural, ethnic, or gender differences
- a values clash.

Managers who have the best intentions and want to address resistance responsibly still tend to focus their efforts on giving more information. Even though more information and communication cannot hurt, it does not address levels 2 or 3.

It is interesting to note that many believe resistance is a natural occurrence. If this is true, change agents need to understand resistance and identify tools and techniques to manage it. William Bridges, the change expert and author of *Managing Transitions*, says that leaders will be more successful if they provide the workforce with these four Ps when introducing change:

- Purpose or the reasons for the change.
- Picture of the expected outcome.
- Plan for navigating from the current situation to the future.
- Part the employee will play in making the changes successful.

Change can bring out the best and the worst in people. Consider Bridges's four Ps when you plan your next change strategy. The CHANGE Model builds actions into the design that address the 4 Ps. The Employees Speak Up exercise, activity 10 in chapter 11, will help your organization identify why resistance might be occurring.

Peter Block, the author of *Flawless Consulting*, believes that resistance is predictable, natural, and a necessary part of the learning process. He believes that resistance is a reaction to an emotional process. And although he is speaking of a consultant-client relationship, his advice is solid. He states that people want to use logic and data to "overcome resistance," as if resistance were an adversary. He notes that you cannot "talk people out of their resistance" because resistance is an emotional process. You cannot talk people out of how they feel. He advocates three steps to handle resistance:

1. Identify in your own mind what form the resistance is taking.
2. Name the resistance using neutral words.
3. Be quiet and allow the person to respond.

You might also consider examining change from a positive experience, such as moving to a new job, buying a new home, getting married, or graduating from college. These events involve the same kind of endings, beginnings, and ambiguity. These events expect you to change old habits, learn new skills, and change the vision of your future. So why don't you resist these changes? There are probably many, and most send a message to leadership about what they can do better to manage employees' transitions during change. (The following was inspired by an activity designed by Kris Taylor.) Consider these:

- You chose the change; therefore, can leaders find ways that allow employees to make choices?
- You were involved in the action; therefore, can leaders find ways that get employees involved in the action?
- Rituals and customs help to transition events such as weddings and graduations; therefore, how can leaders use rituals to honor the past and celebrate the future of the organization?
- Getting married, moving into a new home, going on a vacation are all seen as more desirable; therefore, can leaders help employees view why the preferred future is more desirable for them?

Examine resistance from all perceptions:

- Where it manifests itself from (information, emotions, or personal)
- Employees' needs
- Believing it is an emotional process
- Lessons learned from positive change experiences.

Navigate Doubts: A Tool to Address Resistance

Kurt Lewin viewed situations as being affected by "a sea of forces in motion." Some of these forces are positive and desirable, while others are negative and undesirable. These forces are in constant motion and produce stability or, in Lewin's words, "quasi-stationary equilibrium."

Force field analysis is a useful concept to help identify the forces at work to produce stability or the status quo. Imagine that the center line in figure 6-3 is the status quo. Various forces have an impact on the status quo, pushing from opposite sides to hold it firmly in place. If the driving forces are favorable to the intended change and the restraining forces are those that prevent change, the key is to identify both kinds of forces, strengthen the driving forces, and weaken the restraining forces.

You want the center line to move to the right because it means that the driving forces are stronger than the restraining forces and you are getting closer to your goal. Activity 11 in chapter 11 presents an opportunity to practice using this tool.

Overcoming Resistance to Change: Get Them on the Bus

Even though we can predict human reactions with some degree of accuracy, an effort as big and complex as change cannot be addressed with a one-size-fits-all strategy. Change is personal, and resistance to change is usually an attempt to maintain the status quo. Resistance can slow or stop the organization's

Figure 6-3. Force Field Analysis

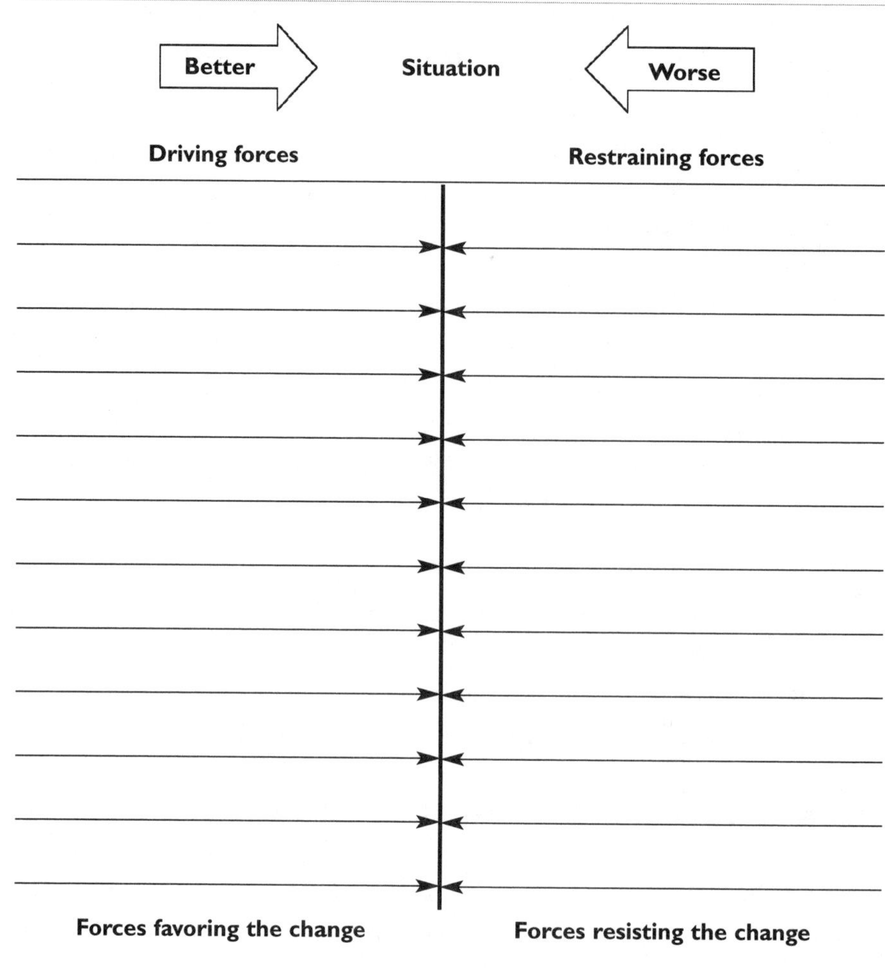

transition to the preferred future. As a change agent, acknowledge the inevitability of resistance and develop a plan for dealing with it. These suggestions could focus on all levels in the organization:

- Identify specific reasons for resistance, and act upon what you learn. It may be a misunderstanding, a fear of loss, a lack of trust, or a concern for having the skills to do what is required. Take corrective action as soon as possible.
- Ensure that everyone understands the proposed changes and that there are no misunderstandings about *what* the organization is doing or *why* the organization is engaged in this effort.
- Always be candid about the possible adverse effects of change.
- Create forums for open, honest, two-way communication. Listen to the feedback and act on it immediately when required.
- Provide management and leadership development for planning, implementing, and monitoring change. Some may not have been through a change effort before and may not appreciate the need to communicate, address resistance, and gain commitment.

- Provide opportunities to celebrate and reward small successes and those who are responsible. This sends a powerful message that the change is important and those who have helped are valuable.
- Do not assume that everyone is on board. You may not have uncovered the strongest resisters.
- Focus on the problem, not the person.
- Consider providing stress management training to assist individuals in coping.
- Help employees say "good good-byes" so they can say "good hellos." It is important to accept the discouragement or sadness that employees may be feeling. Use a ritual or ceremony, even if it is as simple as telling stories about the past and acknowledging how important it was.
- Recognize that "survivors" in a downsizing may feel guilty, distrustful, or depressed.
- Offer training and education to anyone who is facing tasks that he or she has not done in the past. Training reduces stress by increasing self-confidence.
- Create many opportunities for involvement and don't turn anyone down. People advocate what they create.
- And finally, continue to communicate. Use this five-step process to SHIFT resistance (from ebb associates inc, 2004):

  Surface the resistance by making it safe to express it; listen carefully and be certain that you understand the root cause.

  Honor the resistance by affirming the person's right to resist; reassure that you understand, letting the person know that you appreciate the insight.

  Identify the kind of resistance; differentiate between current resistance and former grudges, resentment, or a need for attention.

  Find out what the resister would prefer and begin to work toward a common objective. Check the status to learn if any agreement has been reached.

  Thank the person and move on. You will not be able to eliminate all resistance, though this SHIFT process often works.

Buying In: Taking the Vision Trip from Compelling to Common

Resistance decreases naturally once buy-in to the vision occurs. You may have the utmost compelling vision, but if it doesn't become *everyone's* compelling vision, it will languish on employees' desks, eluding the role it was created for. A vision is much more than just words on a piece of paper; a vision gives people a higher state to aspire to. Employees work better together when they share a vision. So reaching a shared vision, a common vision, is more important than creating it. To go from compelling to shared vision requires some planning. You will be on the right track if you get maximum involvement right from the start.

Create the right vision. No one can be sure whether earlier versions of your vision are correct. It will be the *right* vision, however, if it is flexible enough to adapt to the changing environment.

Get involvement in the creation. Get people involved right from the start. Be sure to invite formal as well as informal leaders to participate in its creation. Once you have a draft vision, share it with key leaders across the organization and ask them to introduce it to their employees. Ask them to critique it and provide feedback. Accept the feedback and adjust the vision appropriately. (See activity 12 in chapter 11.)

Winning Idea:
Have you ever thought about why it is important to repeat the vision often? You may have just remembered repeating your multiplication tables in grade school and thought it was the best way to learn (not true, as a matter of fact). The reason is just buying air time. The average employee takes in about 3 million words or numbers per quarter. If the vision is shared once in a speech or in a couple of emails, each event averages 2,000 to 13,000 words and the market share is less than 1 percent. One of my clients put their change message on a CD and sent it to employees' homes. The idea was well received by the families.

Make the vision easy to communicate. A picture is worth a thousand words, so why not paint a picture or create a graphic that clarifies the vision. You can paint the vision in other ways as well by talking about it with the help of examples or analogies. This will also make it easier to communicate and to remember.

Make the vision easy to adopt as one's own. Can workforce members picture themselves in the vision? Will they be able to participate in the planning? Do they understand why the change is occurring? Do they understand how they fit and what they can do?

Communicate the vision in many ways. Repeat the message. Remember, people need to hear it seven times before they really understand the full meaning. Present the vision in multiple forums: every meeting, written messages, newsletters, podcasts, listening posts, town hall meetings, award ceremonies, posters, CD-ROMs, and hundreds of other ways. It seems like a blinding flash of the obvious, but be sure to integrate the vision into the communication plan.

Make the communication two-way. Create opportunities for dialogs. Listen first, last, and in between to allow employees to work out their personal concerns with the change. Make it easy for supervisors to discuss the vision to create a natural discussion about the vision. Provide them with talking points.

Lead by example. Nothing, but nothing, is more powerful than modeling the vision to gain respect, credibility, and support for the effort. Align all organizational actions and decisions.

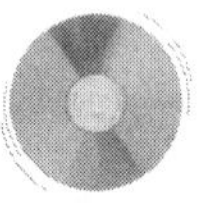

You will want to assure buy-in from every employee. The Employees' Success Guide to Change in appendix B will help. Customize the guide on the CD-ROM and distribute it to all your employees.

Checklist for Step 3: Activate Commitment

- ❑ Teams have been identified for planning and implementation.
- ❑ Expectations are being managed.
- ❑ The implementation plan has been designed.
- ❑ Planning meetings have been held.
- ❑ The communication plan has been implemented.
- ❑ A process is in place to update the communication plan.
- ❑ Implementation reports and documents have been designed.
- ❑ The implementation plan including key milestones has been presented to key individuals for their buy-in.
- ❑ A stakeholder chart has been created.
- ❑ A strategy has been developed to bring key players on board.
- ❑ Involvement is encouraged:
    - — Suggestions have been requested from employees.
    - — Everyone has been involved that should be involved.
    - — The case for change has been communicated and understood.
    - — Employees have been scheduled for the necessary training and preparation.
    - — Management is assisting people to align with the change.
- ❑ Leadership understands reactions to change.
- ❑ Management has explored resistance to change.
- ❑ A force field analysis has been used to determine restraining and driving forces.
- ❑ Strategies for overcoming resistance have been discussed with key players.
- ❑ Supervisors have practiced the SHIFT resistance model.
- ❑ The Employees' Success Guide to Change has been distributed to appropriate employees (see appendix B and CD-ROM).

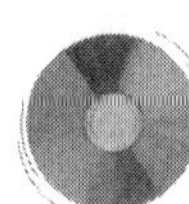

Chapter 7

Nurture and Formalize a Design (Step 4)

The key to everything is patience. You get the chicken by hatching the egg, not by smashing it.

—Arnold Glasow

In This Chapter:

- Understanding how change has an impact on the system
- Revisiting and refining metrics
- Managing risk: conducting a risk assessment
- Tools for implementation and planning

People have to believe your organization is dead serious about this change effort and that leadership is willing to do whatever it takes to make it successful. Pat McLagan states that "65 percent of all changes are considered failures. A large percentage of the rest fail to meet all expectations" (*T+D*, December 2002). Leaders must be ready to put the energy required into making the change successful.

Even though you have created an implementation plan, you will still need to ensure alignment within the system and that the planned solutions support the ultimate goal. And speaking of success, you will need metrics to measure

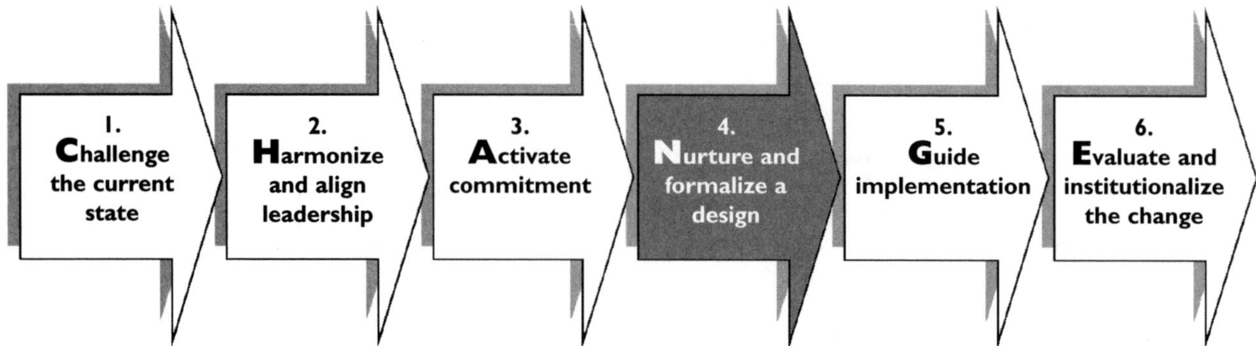

the success and a risk management plan to ensure that if any stumbling blocks appear you have a plan to mitigate the problems. Taking a deep dive into your organizational systems before conducting a risk assessment is a practical thing to do because you will have more knowledge about the systems and the things that could go wrong. Implementation and planning tools are also introduced here. You may have used some of them in the design of the implementation, but it is more likely that you may use them here to maintain a semblance of organization! Let's begin by examining the system in which the change is taking place.

How Change Has an Impact on the Whole System

You examined the systems in the last step when designing the implementation plan. Because it was one of a dozen things you had to address, chances are you took a somewhat superficial look at all the processes within the system. Now is the time to establish a deep understanding of how each of the processes undergoing change will affect the other processes in your system. Identify and alter any structures, processes, or procedures that may undermine the change effort.

Winning Idea:
Remember that red, 600-page *Fifth Discipline Fieldbook* you used to carry around in the 1990s? Time to pull it off the library shelf again. You have to understand systems to be successful with change. And nobody does systems better than Peter Senge.

In the last step, you designed the change implementation. You will need to examine your design and ensure that obstacles have been removed from the organizational system that may impede success. This is one of those actions that is not easily pinned down to one step. Your change leader may have thought of the systems changes that need to occur in Step 1, and the design teams will most likely have reviewed systems in Step 3. What are the actions to consider as you nurture the change?

Look at all the parts of the system that the change will affect and make sure that you have considered them in the design. McLagan tells us that preparing the system for change is one of the most essential steps you must take: "A recurring theme in the world's change research is the importance of adjusting various aspects of the organization so that the change can take root and thrive. A change may require minor or radical shifts in processes, technology, tools, information flows, skills, structures, facilities, and so on" (*T+D*, December 2002). You may want to examine and/or adjust some of these:

- Processes, both primary and those related that need to change.
- Procedures that are a part of the processes that changed and the standard operating procedures that support them.
- Pay and benefit systems, and other recognition efforts to support the new design.
- Selection and hiring efforts to bring people on board with the required competencies.
- Information technology systems that support the change either directly or peripherally.
- New employee orientation and other training efforts.
- Support for supervisors and managers, because they hold the organization together during times of change.
- Recruiting for the new, changed skill set.

Winning Idea:
It is interesting to note that high-performing companies link pay to performance. A study published in the July 2003 *Harvard Business Review* reported that 90 percent of high-performing companies link pay to performance, while only 15 percent of low-performing companies did the same. What have you done to link pay to performance in your plans?

People and Systems

You've looked at the various systems that make up your organization. Don't forget about the workforce. In his book *Managing at the Speed of Change*, Daryl Conner says, "I want to caution you here about the trap into which many people fall when introducing change. If you haven't built a comprehensive picture of the total assimilation drain on the people affected by multiple changes, you may be seduced into thinking that a particular project will be assimilated without much of a problem." You've been there—change is coming at you in all directions. Sometimes the changes are competing across departments. Sometimes the changes are competing for resources within departments. One thing is for sure: The changes are always competing for time. Three points are important here:

- Even the best implementation plan will struggle if it is poorly timed.
- Employees in many organizations feel overworked. Introducing change adds to their stress level and their workload.
- Employees deal with competing priorities. Introducing change will add to the difficulty of deciding how to use their time.

"Change-fatigued" is the term one of my clients has coined to describe the multitude of change her people have been through during the past year. What efforts have occupied the members of your organization's workforce during the past couple of years? Ask them. Take time to map these efforts. You may be surprised at the number, variety, and sources.

Updating Plans as a Result of Examining the System

Once you have completed your systems analysis, you'll have a better appreciation of how the various processes, departments, and locations affect each other. This is a good time to examine the implementation plan you designed in the last step. Ask these questions:

- What processes need to be aligned with the new design?
- Who is the likely candidate to assume responsibility for this alignment process?
- How will we begin to change the process?
- When shall we begin?

Also, remember the communication plan that was developed in Step 3? It is time to pull it out now and add more specifics. Have the timeline and milestones been affected? Does the plan involve opinion leaders? Which stakeholders have a different role? Have you created new signs and symbols, rites and rituals that remind everyone of the change?

Revisiting and Refining Metrics

Although you identified measures that indicate success when you developed the implementation plan, it's time to take a second look to confirm that the metrics chosen will be the driving force toward the desired future. A metric is intended to be used as a tool to reflect what is important to an organization. Metrics say as much about the organization as anything. The "metrics messages" are not always clear, and more often they are not consistent. Even worse, employees sometimes misinterpret the measures. Sometimes it is difficult to construct meaningful metrics for a large change intervention because there are many important attributes. If you have had difficulty constructing meaningful metrics, turn to activity 14 in chapter 11.

Metrics go beyond simply operationalizing important performance indicators; they become the driving factors of how the designers envision the organization's preferred future. To attain buy-in for the metrics—and thus the "preferred future"—an implementation team may present a draft of the metrics to the leadership for approval. This might be done at high-level leader meetings, engaging leadership in conversations about implementation and what is embodied in the metric—both measurement and goal.

An organization considers these questions when developing metrics:

- What individual and organization-wide behaviors are the metrics intended to reinforce?
- How will the metric information be used? For what purpose? Who will receive the information, in what format, and how often?

- What organizational output and/or performance will be measured?
- How will data be collected and analyzed?
- How will the metrics be linked to the reward process?

Metrics should be realistic, meaningful, timely, and exacting. They should support the change vision by rewarding new behavior, and they should provide concrete proof of success. They should be incorporated into other metric systems the organization uses, such as a balanced scorecard. Whatever metrics are chosen for the effort, they should

- support the strategic direction
- ensure that the information reaches the right people in a timely manner
- be easy to track, not requiring (if possible) a surrogate process and additional administrative work to "count"
- provide ongoing input to drive timely, responsive actions.

The organization may be looking for long-term, midterm, and immediate metrics.

Long-term metrics. An organizational assessment provides long-term measures. It may be used to assess employee satisfaction of the change effort and successful organizational "culture" changes. An organizational assessment may be conducted every two to five years, though some organizations conduct an annual organizational assessment, such as an employee satisfaction survey.

Midterm metrics. Most organizations have a system for measuring progress. Many use a balanced scorecard process to provide a way to measure annual goals. Whatever your organization uses, you will need something to track the progress of the change effort objectives on a frequent basis—usually monthly or in six- to eight-week intervals.

Immediate metrics. Metrics built into daily processes provide measures that can be tapped into on demand. The caution with this comes from W. Edwards Deming to ensure that individuals are not tampering with the process when they see data that are clearly in control but may not be what the manager wants to see. These immediate measures cascade down from the measures identified in an organization's annual measurement plan, for example, a balanced scorecard.

Certainly, the more precise and quantifiable the goals are, the easier it is to assess whether they have been met. You can rely on the common SMART model for writing Specific, Measurable, Attainable, Realistic, Time-bound goals. Change effort metrics have a twist. You will find in the next chapter (Step 5) that metrics should also be concrete proof that the change effort is successful and that they reward new behaviors.

Test your metrics against the criteria in this acronym that spells METRICS. Your change effort metrics should be

Meaningful and trusted by upper management

Exacting, so they can be counted and you'll know if things are getting better or worse

Timely, to prevent delays in reviewing them

Rewarding for new and changed behaviors

Intended for all workforce members

Concrete proof of success

Supportive of the change vision, in both the short and long terms.

A change effort metrics example. This is an example of how one organization intended to measure the success of its change intervention. Its key metrics include:

- The Delta Organization has the ability to maintain a pipeline of qualified employees so that there are no gaps in the "key positions."
- One hundred percent of employees have an active Individual Development Plan by December 20XX that incorporates rotational assignments, mentoring, and other career-expanding opportunities.
- The Delta Organization has developed a structure and governance plan for mentoring and rotational assignments by December 20XX.
- The Delta Organization has designed and is testing a draft succession planning process by September 20XX.
- The Delta Organization has completed competency management system pilots in finance, contracts, and manufacturing by June 30, 20XX.
- The Delta Organization conducts a strategic planning session that aligns all departments and measures its success using a balanced scorecard approach in 20XX.
- A new personnel system is implemented with a limited amount (3.5 on a scale of 5) of dissatisfaction among employees and supervisors by December 20XX.
- The Delta Organization has established a practical orientation for new employees, which all attend within six days of starting their jobs.
- Identified departments have written diversity plans in place using the assistance of a diversity coordinator by June 20XX.
- The Delta Organization has piloted its "Academy of Learning" and has placed 30 percent of employees through the process by September 30, 20XX.
- The Delta Organization has reduced the amount of time to bring employees on board by 50 percent by December 31, 20XX.

Managing Risk: Conducting a Risk Assessment

It is difficult to plan precisely for many of the changes experienced in organizations today. These transformational changes are so big, so dramatic, and so hard to manage that there is often some uncertainty about what to do and how to do it. In addition, external events may be out of your control. These are just two reasons why it is important to conduct a risk assessment.

A risk assessment is a tool that you can use to help manage the risk that accompanies any change intervention, but especially a transformational change. A number of techniques address the phases of risk management. But first, what is risk?

Risk is a measure of the potential inability of an organization to achieve its objectives as planned. It has two components:

- the probability or likelihood of failing to achieve the plan as intended
- the consequence or impact of failing to achieve the planned outcome.

Risk management is the process of dealing with the risk involved when planning an event. The steps include identifying potential risks, analyzing areas of risk, developing options, and monitoring and addressing risks as they change. Implicit in the definition is that risks are future events—potential problems—and that there is uncertainty about the success of the change if the identified risks occur. Therefore, there is a need to estimate the probability and the impact.

The Process for Managing Risk

An easy but effective process to manage risk is presented here in four steps. The first step is *risk identification*, which you begin by compiling a list of all the potential things that can occur to prevent achieving the outcome of the change effort. This can be completed by asking a group of informed people to brainstorm (or use other idea-generating tools) these risks. If the change management effort is very large, you may wish to conduct one with each of the implementation teams. You may also use expert interviews, process examination, reviewing past lessons learned, or other activities that generate a list of items that could go wrong.

Winning Idea:
Looking for some fabulous question for identifying risks or brainstorming other concerns. Dan Cohen's book *The Heart of Change Field Guide* has numerous lists of great questions—just right for stimulating discussions.

The second step, *risk analysis*, begins with an examination of the risk events that have been identified, as well as the performers that will be used to determine the impact, such as cost, schedule, quality, customer satisfaction, and others that are important to your organization.

You will need to develop risk ratings, often expressed as high, moderate, and low. It is wise to incorporate definitions such as the examples given in table 7-1. Use definitions that address your unique needs. Each of the identified risks will be compared with these scales, and the scales will be placed on a grid to graphically display where the greatest risks might occur. Figure 7-1 is an example.

The third step, *option development,* requires you to identify the root causes and mitigating strategies that will minimize the risks if they happen. Again, depend on your teams of experts to assist with this step.

There will not always be a clear distinction between the first three steps because it is difficult to cleanly separate the steps—and it isn't always necessary to keep the process that sterile. For example, if a risk is identified by an implementation team, it is natural to discuss the probability and the impact. This discussion may naturally lead to ways to address the risk. Capture these discussions separately so that you do not lose the ideas. Use the ideas to complete an option development chart like the one in Table 7-2.

The fourth step is to *monitor and address risks* as they change. This requires that someone be assigned to champion the risk management process; or if it is a large change effort, the risks may be assigned to various individuals. As the design unfolds, the responsible individuals ensure that strategies that prevent the risk from occurring are implemented as needed.

Contingency Planning

You may also want to introduce a simpler process to prepare for what may go wrong. In contingency planning, a group identifies possible things that could go wrong (such as those in chapter 4) and identifies how to prepare for them. Several examples are given in table 7-3.

Should you ever abandon the plan? Heresy! Never, never give up! But in fact you *may* end a project. It is possible that you will cut your losses and stop the change initiative. Although this is rare, it does happen on occasion. In some instances, the accelerating rate of change may have overtaken the current change. In other cases, it may be due to something totally unforeseen. This happened to many organizations after 9/11.

Table 7-1. Sample Risk Ratings with Definitions

	Probability of Risk Occurring		Impact
1	Remote	1	Minimal
2	Unlikely	2	Acceptable; able to meet dates
3	Likely	3	Acceptable; slip in key milestones
4	Highly Likely	4	Acceptable; critical-path impact
5	Near Certainty	5	Unacceptable; can't meet key customer dates

Figure 7-1. Risk Assessment: The Risk-Level Chart

Impact

Impact										
10			Finance Testing				Network	New Versions		Data Conversion
9			Budget Execute							
8					Data Val. Turnover					
7							Business Changes			
6										
5										
4										
3								Regain Momentum		
2			Smaller Network Needs							
1										
	1	**2**	**3**	**4**	**5**	**6**	**7**	**8**	**9**	**10**

Probability

Probability		**Impact**	
1–2	Remote	1–2	Program objectives unchanged
3–4	Not likely	3–4	Minor impact on people and process
5–6	Possible	5–6	Reduced capability; still mission-capable
7–8	Highly expected	7–8	Significant; affects ability to obligate funds
9–10	Near certainty	9–10	Quality and quantity reduced; unable to meet organizational requirements

Table 7-2. Risk Assessment: Option Development

Rollout Risk	Risk-Rating Ratio*	Root Cause for Risk	Mitigating Strategies
1. Data conversion, clean-up translation	10:10	Bad data; huge unknown	Users review data in system; run queries periodically for missing or invalid data. Point of contacts in each business area to help with data. During data conversion, assign dedicated resources to fix data problems.
2. New versions create unfixable system problems, complexities, patches	8:10	Constant product upgrades to provide more functionality; COTS life	Finish development of older version so it is ready for deployment, as a backup. Redirect resources to work 11.5.10. Utilize resources from other departments to input data as a work around to get enough data to do reports. Work with vendor for solutions to the system problem, determine if patches are necessary. Modify Business Process to be more in line with application.
3. Remote access/network	7:10	Servers were moved; current problem is lack of expertise to configure hardware and software	System is a nonstarter without this addressed. Need fresh eyes to look at our problem. Spend the money to get the expertise to obtain the proper configuration of the remote network connectivity. Invest in dedicated point-to-point communication solution between NR and the remote site for a better, faster, and more reliable connectivity option; requires management support. Recommend high-level person get involved to expedite the point-to-point solution.
4. Major changes in functionality/requirements (business process/management redirection)	7:7	Priorities; management structure	Finalize the reorganization; there is a limited understanding of how the changes affect the process. Can establish a cut-off date and freeze any management decisions after that date. Could identify a priority list of things to do after. Need management support to allow the ITC to prioritize the list.

*Ratio is probability to impact.

Table 7-3. Sample Contingency Planning

Contingency: What May Go Wrong	How to Prepare for It
Supervisors are unable to communicate the change to employees properly	Ensure that coaching and training are available; if that fails, be prepared to replace the supervisors
Training is inadequate in quality and quantity	Utilize consultants to assess and deliver as quickly as possible
Senior leader is not available to review and sign off on next steps	Have a decision team sanctioned by the leader to make decision in his or her absence
People continue to use old legacy systems instead of new software	Begin to systemically remove old systems so that there are no other options
Implementation falls behind schedule	Identify root cause; reinvigorate management tools; outsource some work to make up some time

Some organizations have a "kill point" where they have decided that if something does or does not occur they will stop the effort. This is not common practice, however. Try to consider as many risks as early as possible.

Tools for Implementation and Planning

This CHANGE step requires that you make the transition from the planning step to the roll-up-your-sleeves and implement step. Several project management tools and resources can help you stay organized: Gantt charts, PERT charts, action mapping, and role/responsibility matrixes. Let's look briefly at each.

Gantt charts. The Gantt chart is a visualization tool commonly used by project managers to control and administer the sequence of steps required to complete a task. Developed by Charles Gantt in 1917, they are also known as horizontal bar charts, milestone charts, and activity charts. They are useful for planning, coordinating, and scheduling the steps necessary.

Each step on a Gantt chart is represented as a single horizontal bar on an X-Y chart. The horizontal axis (X axis) is the time scale over which the task will endure. Therefore, the length of each step bar corresponds to the duration of the step, or the time necessary for completion. On a more complex chart, arrows connect independent steps to reflect the relationships between the steps. These relationships usually show dependency, where one step cannot begin until another is completed. The resources necessary for completion may also be listed next to the chart. The Gantt chart is an excellent tool for quickly assessing the status of a project.

To construct a Gantt chart, identify all the steps necessary to complete a task and how much time will be required. List these steps on the left side of the chart in sequential order and draw a bar to represent the amount of time required to complete the step. Use the Gantt chart during a change initiative to schedule people, plan training, and request equipment moves at the appropriate time. You may use Microsoft Project to easily create a Gantt chart using typical Microsoft actions similar to those in any Microsoft application (see figure 7-2).

Winning Idea:
An organization I work with posted a variety of change-related tools like those you see here on its intranet. Employees can visit the Talent Management website, click on the change management link, and have direct access to information such as a change management toolkit, change management models, and leading team tools. Employees can also access the business case for the current change effort and minutes of team meetings as well as a schedule of future meetings.

PERT charts. Program Evaluation and Review Technique (PERT) charts were first developed in the 1950s by the U.S. Navy to help manage large, complex projects that had a high degree of intertask dependency. PERT charts are often used to support tasks that are completed in parallel. Microsoft Project can create a PERT chart from a Gantt chart.

PERT charts are used to analyze the events or milestones involved in completing a project. They are especially useful in determining the time needed to complete each event or milestone, and in identifying the minimum time needed to complete the total project. By linking all events or milestones for a project in sequential order and noting their anticipated time for completion, you can determine the "critical path" of the complete project.

The critical path is a series of tasks that must be completed on time for a process to meet its deadline. Most tasks in a typical project have some slack and can, therefore, be delayed a little without affecting the project finish date. Those tasks that cannot be delayed without affecting the project finish date make up the critical path. As you modify actions and timelines to resolve a lack of resources or other problems in your schedule, be aware of the critical tasks. Changes to them will affect your completion date.

Figure 7-2. Example of Gantt Chart

Task	Jan	Feb	Mar	Apr	May	Jun	Jul	Aug	Sep
Interviews	■	■	■						
Questionnaire	■								
Focus groups			■	■	■	■			
Design					■	■	■	■	
Conduct pilot									■

Figure 7-3. Example of PERT Chart Showing Critical Path

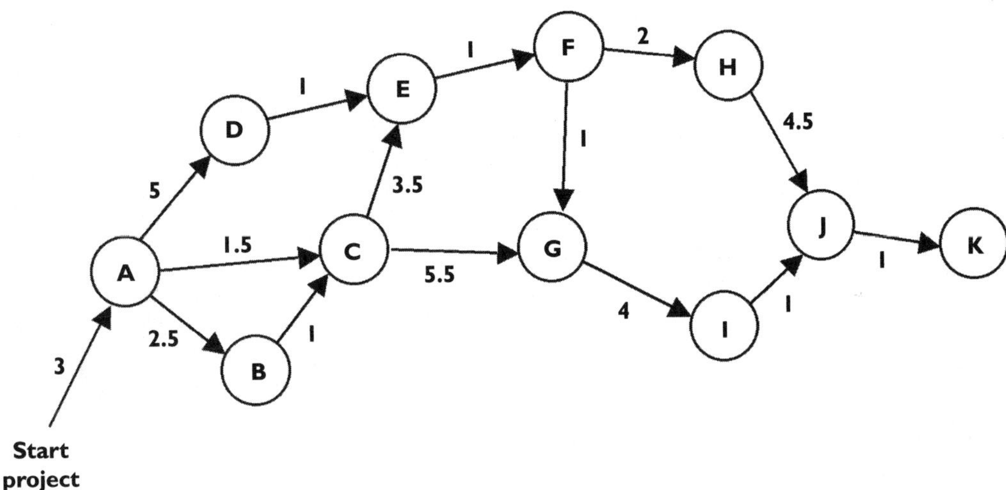

In the sample PERT chart with critical path shown in figure 7-3, it will take three weeks to reach milestone A from the start of the project, 2.5 weeks to accomplish milestone B, and so on. The critical path is the sequence of milestones that if not completed as planned will lengthen the entire project. The critical path of this project is A-B-C-E-F-H-J-K, for a total of 18.5 weeks.

Action map. Action mapping is a process used to clarify what behavior is required from individuals to reach success. It ensures that everyone knows who completes what action, who has what responsibility, who can approve or reject an action, who must be consulted, and who must support the action often with resources. Generally, this plan has been designed and approved by top management. In the sample action map in figure 7-4, each individual is assigned a level of responsibility.

You may find it useful to use different descriptors that work better for your organization. In addition, for complex change, you may find it is useful to have a high-level action map at the executive level as a general implementation guideline and individual maps as you work through several of the implementation paths. These action-mapping responsibilities are explained in figure 7-4.

Role/responsibility matrix. A role/responsibility matrix form is another tool similar to the action map that helps to clarify specific assignments and responsibilities; for an example of this matrix, see figure 7-5. Note that this matrix can be used for individuals as well as departments.

Figure 7-4. Example of Action Map

Action	Samy	Brian	Ono	Dan	Jenna	Maria	Emma	Arnie	
Submit budget	A	E	C	R	C	C	N	N	
Schedule room	N	N	C	A	R	R	R	E	
Hire consultant	R	A	C	C	C	E	N	C	

Key: The letters indicate the level of responsibility each individual is expected to carry out for each task: A = action officer—has responsibility but not necessarily authority; E = endorser—must approve and may reject; R = resource sponsor—must support and provide resources in the form of people or money to complete the action; C = communicate/consult—must be consulted/informed before the action occurs, but cannot refuse; and N = neutral or none.

Figure 7-5. Example of Role/Responsibility Matrix

Task	Wayne	Thad	Omar	Mason	Tarsha	HR
Submit budget	P	S+		C	C	
Schedule room	C	P	S		C	
Hire consultant	V			P	S+	
Develop evaluation format	C	V	C	C		P

Key: P = primary responsibility; S = secondary responsibility; V = able to veto; C = communication (inform before the action). A + means that extra emphasis is required. A blank space means that there is no relationship between the individual and the task.

Checklist for Step 4: Nurture and Formalize a Design

- ❑ The design has been examined, and obstacles have been removed from the system that may impede success.
- ❑ We have examined how the workforce will be affected by the additional workload and changes:
  - — Training in new skills and coaching in new values and behaviors has begun.
  - — Everyone has been encouraged to get involved in the change effort in some way.
  - — Management is prepared to help those who have difficulty making the adjustment.
  - — Rewards have been established for appropriate change.
- ❑ Metrics have been confirmed.
- ❑ Metrics were compared with the METRICS model to ensure they meet the criteria.
- ❑ A risk assessment has been completed.
- ❑ Implementation tools have been developed to keep us organized.
- ❑ We have implemented a monitoring methodology and reporting structure.

Chapter 8

Guide Implementation (Step 5)

Great ideas need landing gear as well as wings.
—C.D. Jackson

Brains, like hearts, go where they are appreciated.
—Robert McNamara

In This Chapter:

- Encouraging involvement
- Building momentum with short-term gains
- Motivational factors

You're making progress: The change implementation design is complete, assignments have been made, teams have been selected. The change effort is well on its way, and you can sit back and watch the action unfold. Right? Wrong! The change agent facilitating the process will be busier during this step than all the rest combined. This is the action step. And your time will be filled.

What will you be doing? The majority of your day will be spent coordinating the numerous and varied activities that others have been assigned. You will ensure that milestones are met and timelines are maintained. No matter how well you plan, all things will not go smoothly. You will find yourself negotiating between different departments and fostering collaboration

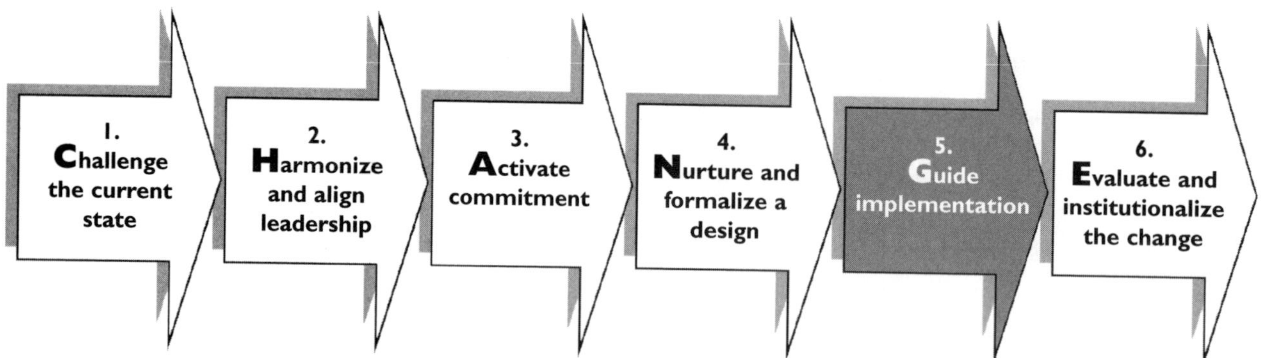

between diverse groups. You may have thought you had commitment from a department head and now find out that you do not. Sometimes people say yes to things, not thinking through completely the effect the change will have; or thinking they will say "yes" and figure out the details later; or even saying "yes" believing that "this will never happen," like past efforts. You will find yourself playing organizational politics and determining how to motivate various employees, managers, and leaders.

Sit back and watch the action? Hardly. You will likely go home some days exhausted, even though you'll wonder what you accomplished or feel as if you have taken a couple of steps backward. There will be many other days when the progress is invigorating and stimulating. It is an exciting time for your organization as you help to guide the implementation. It can be a heady experience and worth all the hard work.

Leading a change initiative requires many roles: designer, integrator, expert, manager, data gatherer, listener, organizer, confidante, collaborator, coach, facilitator, idea generator, realist, timekeeper, logistician, communicator, graphic artist, author. But no role is more important than that of guiding implementation to ensure that it keeps moving forward. And you will find yourself playing all the listed roles in this step. Even though hundreds of details need to be addressed daily, the most valuable efforts will be found in the ways you find to continue to encourage involvement, build momentum, and motivate everyone.

Encouraging Involvement

Guiding implementation is the most activity-laden step in the process. "Good thing it's near the end!" you might be saying. You can lighten your workload by enlisting involvement from all the members of the workforce around you. In doing so, the implementation will go more smoothly and more quickly, too. You can find support in each of these ideas; check them out to speed up the process, to make it Q-U-I-C-K-E-R:

Query executives for sponsorship and support

Update management teams regularly

Implement capacity-building efforts

Create effective transition strategies

Know the informal leaders of the workforce

Engage stakeholders, even those on the fringes

Reach out to the naysayers.

Let's take an in-depth look at each of these ideas to identify several practical tasks.

Query executives for sponsorship and support. The transition period is a complicated time for the organization. In most instances, difficulty will show up here. Some people will be stuck in the old patterns, some will be juggling both the old and new, some will be addressing resistance in their departments, and others may be dealing with the daily crises that arise due to any natural transition. As in football, it is during the handoffs that most errors are made.

Executives can lend their credibility and show their commitment in a number of ways:

- Meet with teams to provide advice and encouragement.
- Lead additional meetings to provide and update and solicit questions.
- Solicit specific individuals who may not yet be fully engaged to help with the transition.
- Provide visible recognition through award ceremonies, letters of congratulations, and other efforts to reinforce appropriate behavior.

Update management teams regularly so they can pass success stories on. Keeping all management informed is critical at this juncture. Depending upon what is happening, weekly, twice weekly, or even daily updates should be the norm. Managers cannot distribute information if they do not have updated content themselves.

Implement capacity-building efforts: seek people from underrepresented groups. How are your administrative staff involved in the change effort? How about the staff who show up for the midnight shift? How about your interns? How have you involved your branch office employees? All these people are part of the workforce but often are not tapped to help implement a change effort. If you are already using them, bravo! If you aren't, think about how you can use them.

Figure 8-1. Weekly Snapshot

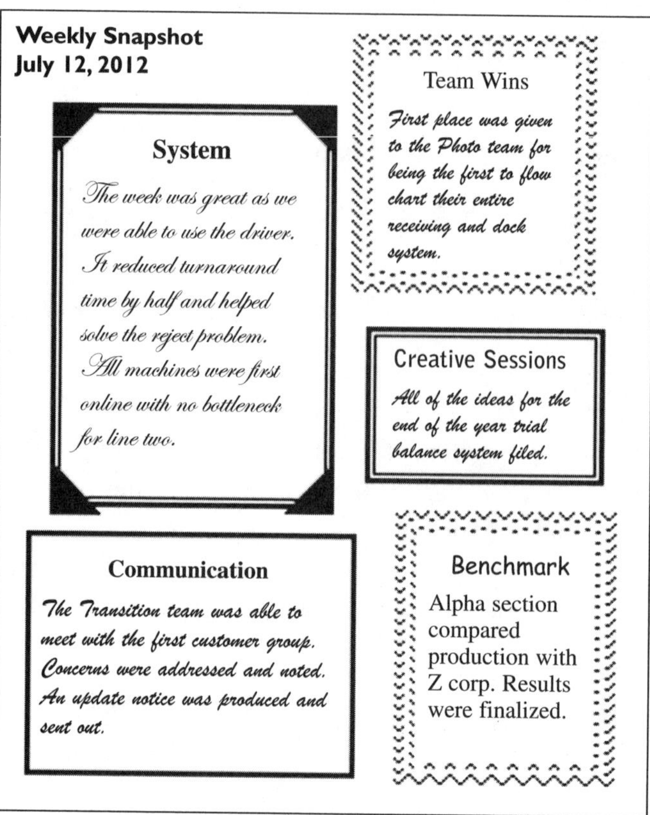

Winning Idea:

One of my clients created an information delivery system that was cascaded down weekly. First, the vice presidents met with the president on Monday and received an outline of the weekly change initiative message. A brief question session followed. Then they received the "Weekly Snapshot" page, the same information in a more complete but snapshot format (see figure 8-1). Each vice president was expected to meet with his or her directors by the end of the day to share the "Weekly Snapshot." The directors were expected to do the same at their weekly staff meetings. This continued down the chain so that everyone had the "Weekly Snapshot" by midweek.

At this point, you should have less ambiguity and more clarity about the tasks that need to be completed but less time to complete them. Getting these groups of folks (and there are probably others in your organization) involved has three important results during the implementation:

1. You are building momentum in other areas of the organization, which can only help to spread the word.
2. You have additional people power to complete the never-ending list of to-dos.
3. You are providing learning experiences and developing the skills of other people who will be ready and better able to help you next time.

This is a win-win for you, the individual, and the organization.

Create effective transition strategies; reevaluate and improve them. As I stated above, handoffs are difficult, whether in a game of football or transitioning a change management initiative. It's the time when someone fumbles the ball. Use this checklist to ensure that you have considered each of these and have someone addressing them:

✓ Processes have been documented and responsibilities for changes have been assigned.

✓ Employee behavior has been clearly defined and documented.
✓ Employee skills and knowledge have been defined; training or other learning experiences have been scheduled.
✓ Management and leadership capabilities have been defined, and appropriate coaching or other methods have been identified.
✓ Conflicting policies and procedures have been revealed, with a champion addressing each.
✓ Communication and the communication plan have been revisited, and weaknesses have been addressed.
✓ A scoreboard is being updated regularly to keep everyone informed about milestones that have been met or are slipping.
✓ All the above tasks are being documented in a regularly updated implementation plan.

Know the informal leaders of the workforce and gain their trust. But how do you build trust? There are four general behaviors that will build and strengthen a trusting relationship:

- Honesty and candor. "I say what I mean." "You will always know where I stand." "You can be straight with me."
- Accessibility and openness. "I'll tell you what works best for me." "Tell me what works for you." "Let's keep our agendas open."
- Approving and accepting. "I value people and diverse perspectives." "You can count on being heard without judgment or criticism."
- Dependability and trustworthiness. "I do what I say I will do." "I keep my promises." "You can count on me."

As positive as each of these trust-strengthening behaviors appears, they can be perceived differently. Here are a few examples:

- Someone who values honesty and candor may perceive carefully chosen "approving and accepting" comments as couched, hiding something, or weak.
- Someone who values accessibility and openness may perceive actions from someone who exhibits "dependability and trustworthiness" as closed, slow, or too cautious.
- Someone who values being approving and accepting may perceive "honest and candid" directness as harsh, insensitive, or uncaring.
- Someone who values dependability and trustworthiness may perceive "accessibility and openness" as flaky, undependable, or unreliable.

What is natural for one person may be very difficult for another. Generally, it is easier to build trust with others who appreciate the same values in building trust as you do. During the change initiative, however, you will be working with people who value trust from all perspectives. Trust is built more easily if you identify what is important to each individual and focus on what that person needs from you to become more trusting of you and your message. You will be more successful in building trust with everyone if you can determine what is important to others and focus on those behaviors.

When building trust, you may need to take the first step toward others. Extend yourself a bit more than is comfortable. Ignore suspicious responses. Mistrust is a form of self-protection and is not easily relinquished. Always, always do what you say you will. Keep your promises—no matter how small. And if you absolutely can't? Call the person as soon as you know, stating how you intend to rectify the situation. Listen! Listen! Listen! Learn what makes each informal leader tick. And reciprocate. Let people in on who you are, too. These may seem like lessons learned in kindergarten. They are. And they work.

Explore your own strengths to build trust alone or with a group using activity 15 in chapter 11.

Engage stakeholders, even those on the fringes. One research group reported by Patricia McLagan in *T+D* (December 2002) stated that people commit to change "to comply, be like others they admire, or to support a change they intrinsically believe in." Find the friends of the change effort and enlist them to help with tasks that are piling up on your desk. Communications could help to write the CEOs' presentations. Finance could help by crunching and displaying some of the data that has come out of the pilot. HR could help develop a recognition system. There are plenty of tasks for everyone.

In addition, identify those people who are on the periphery who can help make things happen. Just because the information technology (IT) system does not affect HR systems directly does not mean that HR will not have to deal with some of the fallout. Keep everyone involved, at least through communications.

For reaching those who are reluctant to join in, here's an idea: One creative change agent sent thank-you notes in advance. She claims that people couldn't resist her request for help.

Reach out to the naysayers. The transition must begin with an ending. Invest time in the naysayers. Do a little investigating. What is behind their negative attitudes? They will not be able to change until they have let go of what they believe they are hanging onto. Perhaps they are resisting letting go of the past—not the change itself.

Over the years, I have conducted many powerful exercises. One of those, shared by Michele Wyman, is called "Holding On and Letting Go." During the exercise, the facilitator does very little in the way of explanation. It is a self-discovery exercise for people who are hanging on to an old grudge, resentment, complaint, or something from the past that they should have released. Participants review the advantages and disadvantages of both holding on and letting go. It creates very interesting discussions. In chapter 11, I share this exercise in activity 16.

Keep in mind that rumors may be preventing people from moving forward. One very creative ASTD group came up with these ideas:

- Use a Dear Abby approach called "Rose Rogers"—who wears, of course, rose-colored glasses
- Post FAQs on the website
- Use a toll-free "fact or fiction" number to ask and to get answers
- Have a Rumor-of-the-Week contest
- Deal with rumors up front by saying "This is what you don't need to worry about."

Winning Idea:

One of my clients was implementing a new IT system. If you've ever been through that experience, you know how even a tiny programming error can create havoc. The IT department wanted to get all the issues on the table so they could prioritize and fix them. They invited the organization to a "Whine and Cheese Party." Cheese, crackers, and sparkling cider were served. The food was great, and the "whining" wasn't bad either! IT got its information, and everyone had fun.

Building Momentum with Short-Term Gains

Building momentum is a good deal easier when you have short-term gains to share with the rest of the organization. Planning for them right from the start—whether in a small test team, an experiment in one department, or a pilot—will give you results that will help sell the initiative to the fence-sitters.

Short-term gains are accomplished early in the implementation phase. They play an important role in the change transformation in several ways:

- They prove that the effort is worth the trouble; there is a payoff.
- The hype provides reinforcement for those who are leading the change effort.
- A short-term win provides something concrete against which leaders can compare their vision for the effort.
- Wins build momentum whenever they occur, but these early ones often come at a time when everyone has worked hard. They give a necessary boost and encourage the fence-sitters to take the plunge.
- A short-term win not only encourages the fence-sitters but also discourages the cynics and resisters.
- Short-term wins provide proof to the C level—CEOs, COOs, CIOs, and the like—if there was doubt in any corner of the executive floor.

How do you define short-term gains?

- They need to be something that is measurable and visible to the entire organization.
- They need to be a clear win for the organization.
- They need to be a part of the change implementation process.

Most important, you need to ensure that the organization knows about the short-term gains:

- Plan for and create improvements that are visible to everyone.
- Recognize and reward people who made the wins happen, and generously include everyone in the circle of winners.
- Refer to the gains in the communication plan.
- Support the gains with easy-to-understand data and "proof."
- Tell stories of the gains to which the workforce can relate.

Finally, is there anything special about organizational culture that you should remember as it relates to short-term gains? Anything about past experiences? Anything leadership has done in the past that either enhanced or deterred the value of the gains? Anything special about celebrating them? Bring a group of change facilitators together to discuss this topic. Better yet, it's a great opportunity for you to "query executives for their sponsorship and support." Schedule 20 minutes to meet with them to obtain their input for the best approach.

Motivational Factors

Too often, change leaders invest time, energy, and money in making a good decision about what to change and how to change but invest very little in building involvement and commitment. If you and the organization's leaders have been wrapped up in the details of the transition mechanics and processes, it is time to pause to ensure that you have truly done everything you can to motivate the workforce.

In the first step of the CHANGE Model, you completed a Change Readiness Predictor for your organization. Because a "supportive culture" was worth only 4 points at the high end of the scale (some factors were worth 12), you may have not paid much attention to it. However, when implementing the change, those 4 points are extremely valuable and necessary toward success. The early short-term gains, discussed in the last section, can initiate motivation where there was none before.

Motivation can come from two very different places. One is positive and supportive of new ideas for a better organization. The other is tangible dissatisfaction with the status quo and an eagerness for something better than what currently exists. A level of fear, nervousness, or discomfort that results in a sense of urgency must exist for this motivation to have any impact.

It isn't unusual for pessimism to occur during the implementation stage. It may be unavoidable. However, by redirecting this negative energy, a change facilitator can turn pessimism into positive motivation. What have you found that contributes to individual behavior change? Here are a few thought starters:

- Discuss how change will help individuals personally; listening to their content but also to their intent. Does their tone of voice give you any clues?
- Use a "what's good about it" scenario. Ask individuals to imagine that the change goes as planned, and even if they currently think it is worthless, what is good about it?
- Release any energy that might be blocking individuals' motivation by asking them to complete sentences such as "I am afraid the change effort will . . ." and "This change will only be successful if . . ."
- Use creativity techniques, such as asking individuals to view the change from the customer's perspective or to view it 10 years from now. What do they see when looking at it from another perspective?
- Check the resources written by Beverly Kaye and Bob Nelson (see the chapter 8 list in the "Further Reading" section in appendix C). Both share hundreds of ideas to motivate employees.
- Develop role plays or critical incidents that are a little on the edge, such as "The CEO called and said we'd better figure out the implementation or we will all be fired!"
- Think about implementing the SHIFT model that was introduced in chapter 6 during the discussion of resistance to change.

Rewards and Motivation

Recently, when I asked Frank, an executive leader, to do something to promote a change effort, he said, "Elaine, I can never turn you down when you ask for something because in the end you appreciate it so much." Have you shown appreciation for all the members of the workforce who are helping to reach the preferred vision? It's often easy to say thank you to those people who help readily—but do you take the time to thank them so that, like Frank, they will always be there for you? It is more difficult to thank those who do something minor in support, thinking, "It's about time!" But thanking them for their small contribution may go further than you think.

Listed here are 88 rewards—ordinary and not so ordinary—that you can give those who are helping to make it happen. This list is not entirely my own. These ideas for rewards have been collected from clients and what I have learned from authors such as Bob Nelson and Bev Kaye, and many have been used to show appreciation to our clients. They will get you started and will also help you to think of your own personal ideas. Remember, motivators and rewards are very personal. What's rewarding to one person may not be to another. So on to the 88 ideas.

Personalized notes. Keep a stack of congratulations and thank-you cards handy to add your personal note. Create your own note cards, such as:

- Above and beyond
- Thanks a bunch (flowers)
- GRRRREAT job (tiger).

Trophies. Trophies can be one-time items, lighthearted in nature, or they may be more serious. You may also have traveling trophies that move from employee to employee that are kept on permanent display.

One-time awards might include:

- Top banana award (a real banana)
- Lemonade award (lemon for turning lemons into lemonade)
- High-flying award (a glider or kite with a personalized note written on it)
- Donut award (Texas-sized donut to portray, "do not" give up)
- "Atta boy" and "Atta girl" printed notepads
- Blue ribbon awards (purchase at card store or make your own)
- Bravo Zulu flags.

Permanent one-time awards might include:

- Plaques for special achievements are always welcome
- Select a pin design for the change effort and give the pins for performing specific acts
- MVP award, accompanied by a ball cap with the change logo.

Permanent traveling trophies and awards might include:

- Chalk one up for ______ (chalkboard hanging in a prominent place)
- Top dog (stuffed toy dog that moves from employee to employee)
- Name a conference room, hallway, or display case after an employee for a time period.

Thank-you items. "Five-and-dime" type items can be kept in your drawer for an "on the spot" thank you. Create a story the first time you give the item away to personalize the award for your employees:

- Compass (you found your way through it)
- Bubble gum or super glue (you stuck to it)
- Crayons (coloring out of the lines, creative idea, or out-of-the-box thinking)
- Lifesavers (you saved the day)
- Stars—brass, glow-in-the-dark, and the like (all-star award)
- Gold paperclips (you're golden)
- Feathers (a feather in your cap for ____)
- Party horns (you should be tooting your horn)

- Tape measure (you more than measure up)
- Golf or tennis balls (you're really on the ball)
- Light bulb (bright idea).

Give your time. Give your time in many ways, such as:

- Helping out during a specific project
- Washing the employee's car during lunch
- Taking the time to use employees' names.

Extra time. None of us have enough free time. Found time is always appreciated. When using time off, be sure to follow approved organizational guidelines:

- Two-hour lunch
- Day off
- An extra break
- Take employee to break (buy coffee or a snack)
- On-the-job sabbatical (protected time to work on a special project).

Food. Food is always welcomed and can be used and delivered in many ways:

- Bring a brown bag lunch for an employee who is working through lunch breaks to complete a task
- Order pizza for those late-night projects
- Provide any snack item
- Give "coffee tokens" from a local coffee shop.

Surprises. Everyone loves a surprise, and this is a way to add fun to work, too:

- Cover the employee's desk with balloons
- Bring a flower or bouquet from your garden
- Blow up a picture of the person to poster size, and post on the door with a personal note
- Have a cartoon drawn of the employee (talented people in every organization)
- Use large chart paper and make a giant thank-you or congratulations card by hand to post on the employees' door for all to see.
- Bring a toy or book for the employee's child
- Take candid pictures of employees; when the time comes you'll have negatives ready to enlarge or turn into a collage or card.

Group awards. Awards can be given to celebrate specific accomplishments or difficult assignments:

- Managers do the cooking and serving at a cookout
- Bring donuts or fruit
- Bring a cake baked by the change leader
- Bring lasagna for lunch
- Schedule monthly cake and coffee party with the change leaders when everyone can discuss how it's going

- Have an ongoing metric display of how well you are doing
- Bell ringer: For special occasions and when something extraordinary happens, walk through the area ringing a bell
- Have a breakfast meeting off site before the craziness of the day begins
- Recognize efforts during weekly staff meetings
- Sponsor a special dress day, for example, football jerseys for "kick-off" day, Hawaiian Day, or jeans day to celebrate the ending of a difficult step in the change effort
- Sponsor a stress relief day: Bring in a lunchtime speaker, and hire someone to give shoulder rubs; the price of admission is to tell one good joke and post a cartoon on the bulletin board
- Give change teams identity from the start: name, logo, T-shirts.

Learning as a reward. Learning new things can be one of the most rewarding things for many employees:

- Attend a trade show or conference
- Visit a customer
- Benchmark another organization for ideas
- Pay professional organization dues
- Attend a class or workshop
- Offer a professional journal or magazine subscription
- Give the employee a book to help him or her learn something new
- Give a book and have it inscribed by the change leader.

Work as a reward. Work as a reward? Yes, one of the reasons people appreciate their jobs the most is due to meaningful work when employees are

- allowed to select projects
- given an opportunity to deliver the status report on the data they gathered
- assigned to a high-profile team
- able to attend a top-level meeting with the change agent
- given personal development time on the job, such as reading.

Tools to make the job easier. Sometimes it's not the job that's the problem; it's that the employee doesn't have everything that's needed to get the job done. What does the employee need that would make the job easier or more satisfying? Perhaps a

- new computer, laptop, or software
- new chair; let employee select it—or at least the color
- cellular telephone or pager
- personal digital assistant.

Enlist others. You cannot be everywhere all the time. Make it easy for everyone to reward each other. Let them know you expect it:

- Get change effort thank-you notes printed that everyone can use
- Put up a bulletin board where employees can thank other employees, post congratulations to each other, or simply say nice things about each other
- Recognize and thank people who recognize others.
- Repeat positive remarks that you hear about employees from others
- Get an "I caught you doing something good card" (could be permanent and passed on).

Formal rewards. Many opportunities exist to gain recognition for your employees:

- Nominate employees for special awards
- Publish an article in the organization newsletter
- Write letters recognizing specific contributions and send a copy to their bosses
- Add a letter about special achievements to an employee's employment file.

Remember to say thank you face to face. And let's not forget *The One Minute Manager* and Ken Blanchard's advice to us:

- Praise people immediately
- Be specific when you tell them what they did right
- Tell people how good you feel about what they did right and how it helps the organization
- Encourage them to do more of the same.

Activity 18 in chapter 11 provides a way to brainstorm a list of ideas tailored to your organization.

Winning Idea:
Looking for more ideas? Check out the website of Bob Nelson (author of *1001 Ways to Reward Employees*) at www.nelson-motivation.com for a hundred more!

Motivating the Leader

Motivating the leader? A leader is leading! A leader should not need to be motivated! Wrong. The leader is human and humans get tired. The leader has probably been in the throes of this change effort longer than—or at least as long as—anyone else. So whether you are the change agent or the leader or both, leaders get tired.

Maintain your enthusiasm. And if you don't feel enthusiastic, don't show it. Many people are looking to you to maintain their own enthusiasm. No one said this was going to be easy.

Leaders: for times when you do not shine. There will be times during the change effort that you will leave a situation wishing you had handled it differently. It might be that you allowed your irritation to show while answering a question during a meeting. You may have come across as pushing too hard when a team briefed you. Combine the six-pack of questions below with some time to reflect and you will be better prepared for the next difficult incident.

Note: If you are the facilitator for the change effort and you observe the leader responding in a way that he or she did not intend, you can use the questions as a coaching tool. Activity 19 in chapter 11 also suggests that you can use this same six-pack of questions to prepare the implementation team for difficult situations:

1. Why are you disappointed in this situation?
2. What negative impact did it have?
3. What do you wish you had done?
4. What can you do to mitigate it now?
5. What do you want to do differently in the future?
6. How will you remember?

Checklist for Step 5: Guide Implementation

- ❑ We have a plan to ensure that the transition is implemented quickly and with quality.
- ❑ Action toward transition is occurring in all parts of the organization.
- ❑ Momentum is building.
- ❑ Short-term gains have been achieved.
- ❑ We have checked all pilots and short-term implementation to uncover all gains.
- ❑ A plan for exploiting short-term gains throughout the organization has been initiated:
  - — It is visible to everyone.
  - — "Proof" of the gains is easy to understand.
  - — People who made the wins happen are rewarded and recognized.
  - — The gains have been built into the communication plan.
  - — Organizational stories about the gain are told.
- ❑ All aspects of motivation have been explored and implemented.

Chapter 9

Evaluate and Institutionalize the Change (Step 6)

Many of the things you can count, don't count. Many of the things you cannot count, really count.
—Albert Einstein

In This Chapter:

- Evaluating the change effort
- Institutionalizing the change
- Reshaping the organizational culture
- Summarizing the CHANGE Model

Step 6 is the final one. This is another one of those steps that some change agents would like to skip. They are tired and want to move on to something different. Don't skip this step. There is a lot to be learned from it and a lot to be gained by your organization. Capturing the lessons learned for your next change effort is well worth the time investment. Involve others in the dialog. How engaged were employees? What was the outcome? What would you do differently next time?

In addition, if you do not pay attention to ensuring that the change has been implemented and is becoming "the way we do business," you will not succeed. People will want to return to the way they were doing it before. Don't let your effort fail now!

Step 6 is also a time to bring closure to your teams and to celebrate successes.

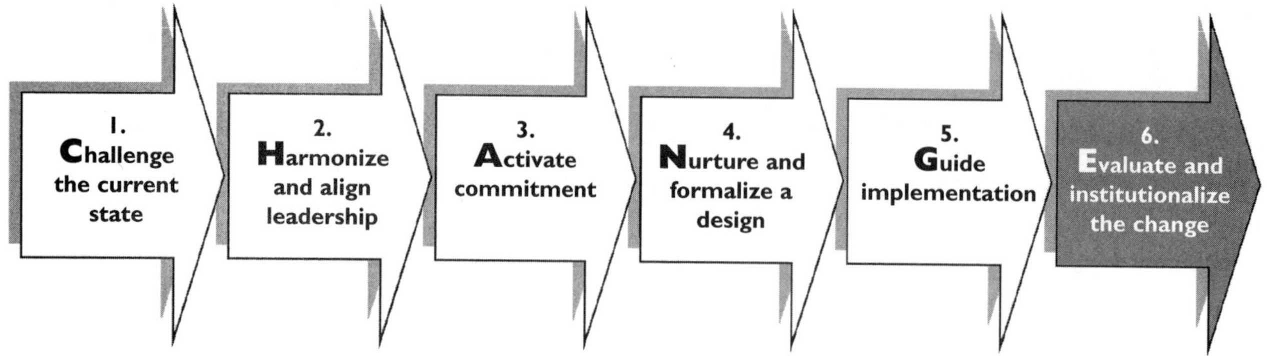

Evaluating the Change Effort

There are many opportunities to evaluate your change effort. Three are presented here: evaluating the impact (did we do what we said we wanted to do), evaluating the process (how well did we do what we did), and evaluating the leader (how well did the leader perform). Each of these allows the organization to learn from mistakes and successes, creating valuable information and lessons learned in preparation for the next change initiative. Without evaluation, managers may not recognize which of their actions contributed to the outcome.

Evaluating the Impact

Was the change effort a success? Evaluating the impact of the change is an important step of closure, but deciding what to do with what you learn is also important. The more people who have been involved in the change effort, the greater the capacity for knowledge sharing and remembering for the next opportunity. So don't take a shortcut during this important step.

Identify whether the change intervention goals were met or not. Activities 20 and 21 in chapter 11 will assist with the evaluation process. Worksheet 9-1 introduces a format for listing goals and whether the organization was successful in achieving them and why (for a full-size version of this worksheet see appendix D and companion CD-ROM). If the goals were not achieved and they have not been overcome by events, the individuals involved in the change effort need to create a contingency plan. What do we do now?

Evaluating the Change Process

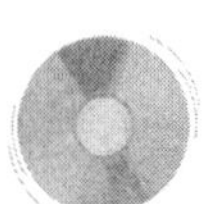

The checklist in worksheet 9-2 can serve as a review of your change intervention (see also appendix D and CD-ROM). How would you rate the process? What lessons did the organization learn? What best practices will you repeat next time? Get a group of people together and follow the directions in activity 21 in chapter 11.

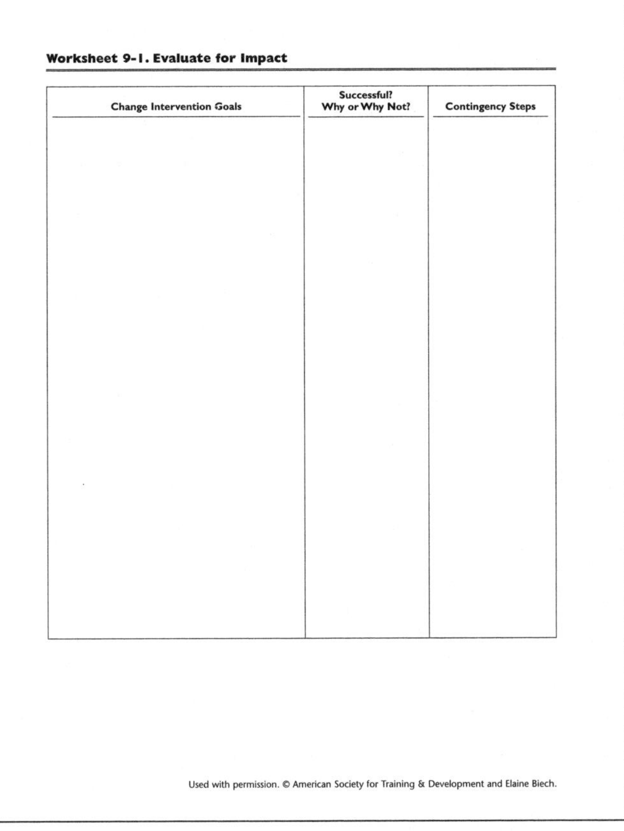

Worksheet 9-1. Evaluate for Impact

Change Intervention Goals	Successful? Why or Why Not?	Contingency Steps

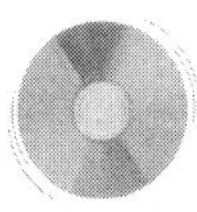

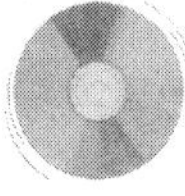

Worksheet 9-2. Evaluate the Change

Event or Action	Failed Miserably	Somewhat Successful	Completely Successful
A solid rationale for change was provided			
Costs were predicted and an adequate ROI was determined			
The leaders of the change were willing volunteers			
A shared vision was created			
Commitment to change was created			
Everyone who wanted to be involved had an opportunity			
The right people were selected for the teams			
A comprehensive implementation plan for the change was prepared			
The change focused on results not activities			
Changes were completed with a minimum of interruption to the workforce			
Customers experienced no interruption of services			
Employees received training, development, and coaching as needed			
The change can be linked directly with the organizational strategic plan			
Monitoring and adjusting occurred in response to problems in the process			
Progress was tracked and published			
Clear success metrics were identified			
Change has been institutionalized with formal policies, systems, and structures			
Top management is committed to continued success of the change			
Employees are pleased with the results			

The best practices and lessons learned that result from this evaluation are those you will want to carry forward to the next change effort. Every organization is different. You may wish to identify other steps in the process that are meaningful to your organization.

Finally, be sure that you have a process in place to store and retrieve the evaluation information. Some organizations use Lotus Notes; others have a dedicated location on the organization's website. Some organizations invest time to bring everyone together to debrief. Others use a format like a report card and track from year to year to ask themselves "Did we really learn those lessons from last year?"

Lessons Learned for Leaders

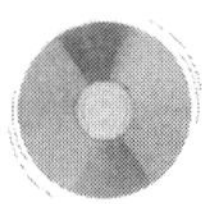

Lessons learned also apply to leaders. Worksheet 9-3 comprises all the actions required of a leader of change (see also appendix D and CD-ROM). Leaders should review and rate themselves to determine what they did well and what things they need to brush up on before the next change effort begins.

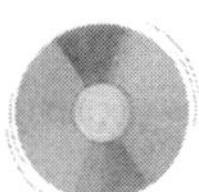

Worksheet 9-3. Lessons Learned for Leaders

Review each of these statements and rate them in the first column using the following scale (and numbers in between): 0 = not at all—must have forgotten; 3 = pretty darn average and I need improvement; 6 = completely—didn't miss a beat.

Add your comments in the third column.

To what extent did you:

0–6	Skills and Behaviors	Comments
	Provide information early and often to employees?	
	Model behavior expected of others?	
	Clearly explain the reason for the change?	
	Focus on results?	
	Help employees understand what's in it for them?	
	Build a team trusted by the organization?	
	Set expectations for continuous change?	
	Create stories and paint a future vision?	
	Engineer some quick wins?	
	Encourage others to participate?	
	Listen to individuals for facts and feelings?	
	Provide all resources required?	
	Give others credit?	
	Provide recognition for small and large wins?	
	Continue to be upbeat and positive?	
	Help to address resistance?	
	Empathize with others' needs and concerns?	
	Manage the transition effectively?	
	Identify ways to symbolize the new identity?	
	Address the change from a systems approach?	
	Find ways to celebrate?	
	Participate in the evaluation?	

What strengths do you think you displayed during the change effort?

Institutionalizing the Change

Many experts in the field of change assert that new approaches are fragile and subject to regression until the changes have a tighter stronghold on the organization's culture. Leaders must make a conscious effort to demonstrate how the changes have improved corporate performance. It is possible to quantify the improvement. For example, Sears created a simple model that helped explain how each individual's personal effort made a direct impact to the bottom line. According to the model, a 5-point improvement in employee attitudes drives a 1.3 percent improvement in customer satisfaction, which then drives a 0.5 percent improvement in revenue (as reported in *Harvard Business Review*, January 1998).

Even with numerical proof, behaviors may revert back, former processes may creep back in, and old familiar relationships may take over. In *The Beauty of the Beast*, Geoff Bellman states that we have "spent years preparing not to change." He suggests that creating dialog on some of these issues is a good way to create awareness and head off regression.

After going through all that you have, you will want to ensure that the change sticks—that it becomes a part of the way you do business. What can you do to ensure that the changes implemented endure and become a part of the culture? John Kotter states that it isn't over until the change has roots. I think it goes beyond roots. I've planted many trees that had perfectly good roots. Without constant care for quite some time, the tree may wither and die.

As with caring for a young tree, you will want to keep the roots of organizational change growing and healthy. That means constant attention for a good amount of time—in some instances, years. Human beings are very good about creating workarounds!

These ideas will help ensure that your change effort continues to grow and become a part of the culture:

- Keep everyone involved in the process.
- Continue to discuss the effort.
- Report on successes—large and small.
- Share and save success stories.
- Reward those who achieved success.
- Remove old ways so that employees have no choice.
- Continue to discuss the benefits of this change.
- Continue to use a communication plan.
- Find new ways to celebrate successes.
- Establish red flags for regressive behavior.
- Articulate the connections between new behaviors and organizational success.

- Ask people for their ideas for refining what has been done, or for ideas about new interventions.
- Use the credibility and success of this effort to address other processes, procedures, roles, and other parts of the organization that do not align with the vision.
- Create a culture of change by rewarding innovation and risk taking, encouraging managers to be mentors and coaches, allowing people to learn from their mistakes, removing barriers to change, fighting for resources, and ensuring that your people know you trust them.
- Adjust all procedures, pay and benefit systems, and other recognition efforts to support the new design.
- Implement a monitoring plan and assign someone the responsibility to report on it regularly.
- Establish a follow-up plan that focuses on key transition areas.
- Let people go who do not comply.
- Find pleasant ways to remind and reward; for example, one company uses pop quizzes by senior management with Starbucks cards as the prize.

Winning Idea:
Joanne Sujansky has written a great little book called *The Keys to Putting Change in Your Pocket.* It sells for under $7, can be carried in your pocket, and helps people work through change. One of the reasons your employees will like it is because it is useful for both professional and personal change. You can purchase copies at www.keygroupconsulting.com. And check out the other change products while you're there.

Reshaping the Organizational Culture

The culture is the organization's personality, reflecting the beliefs, behaviors, and assumptions acquired over time that provide employees with a sense of organizational identity. Culture runs deep. Behavioral change due to a change effort will not change the culture. It may "help" the change or be one factor that "leads to" change or have an effect on the change. But behavior alone will not change the culture. What makes up the culture?

- values
- mission, vision, and goals
- rewards, incentives, and punishment
- history and heritage
- communication lines
- signs, symbols, rites, and rituals
- management style
- organizational gatherings
- organizational structure
- legends, stories, and myths
- company heroes and heroines
- slogans.

With so many signs, both inward and outward, discussed and avoided, you can see why a culture is difficult to change. Many authorities believe it takes at least seven years for a culture to change significantly.

The foundation for a change in the culture is laid when some of the earliest decisions are made about the change effort. How much employees buy into the "new" culture has a chicken-and-egg relationship with the change effort. The foundation for a new culture can be laid by explaining the preferred future and what the change will be. But employees must change their actions to create the new culture. On the one hand, culture is important because it shapes employees' behaviors. And on the other hand, we rely on employees' behaviors to achieve the organization's strategy and to help shape the culture.

Embedding new behaviors in a culture is difficult when the two are consistent. It's even a greater challenge when a difference exists between the behavior and culture. You can see that culture plays a big role in whether the change "sticks" . . . and if it sticks, it will have an effect on the culture.

Although there are pulls and tugs between change and the culture, the culture will always win out. That is why it is the last step in the change effort. You can't coerce a cultural change. You can't manipulate it. You can't shape it without employees' behaviors. Even so, you need to be aware of the organization's culture to wisely plan the steps in the change initiative.

Changing the culture needs to start with a change effort that

- identifies cultural barriers and plans for them
- encourages lots of discussion and even more action from senior management
- produces evidence that the change is not only necessary but important for the organization
- results in proof that the new processes and behaviors are superior to the old
- identifies whether some employees may need to leave the organization.

The bottom line: Culture is important. Pay attention to it. The desire for a culture change should not be the key reason you take on a change effort. A changed culture is a by-product of the change.

Summarizing the CHANGE Model

The CHANGE Model can help you stay focused on what may be at times a very messy process. The process creates a road map for you to follow from initiation through evaluation.

Although the process is linear, remember that each step overlaps the next one and that every organization—indeed, every change intervention—will be different. But each step provides you with guidelines for things to remember for maximum success.

Figure 9-1. The CHANGE Model

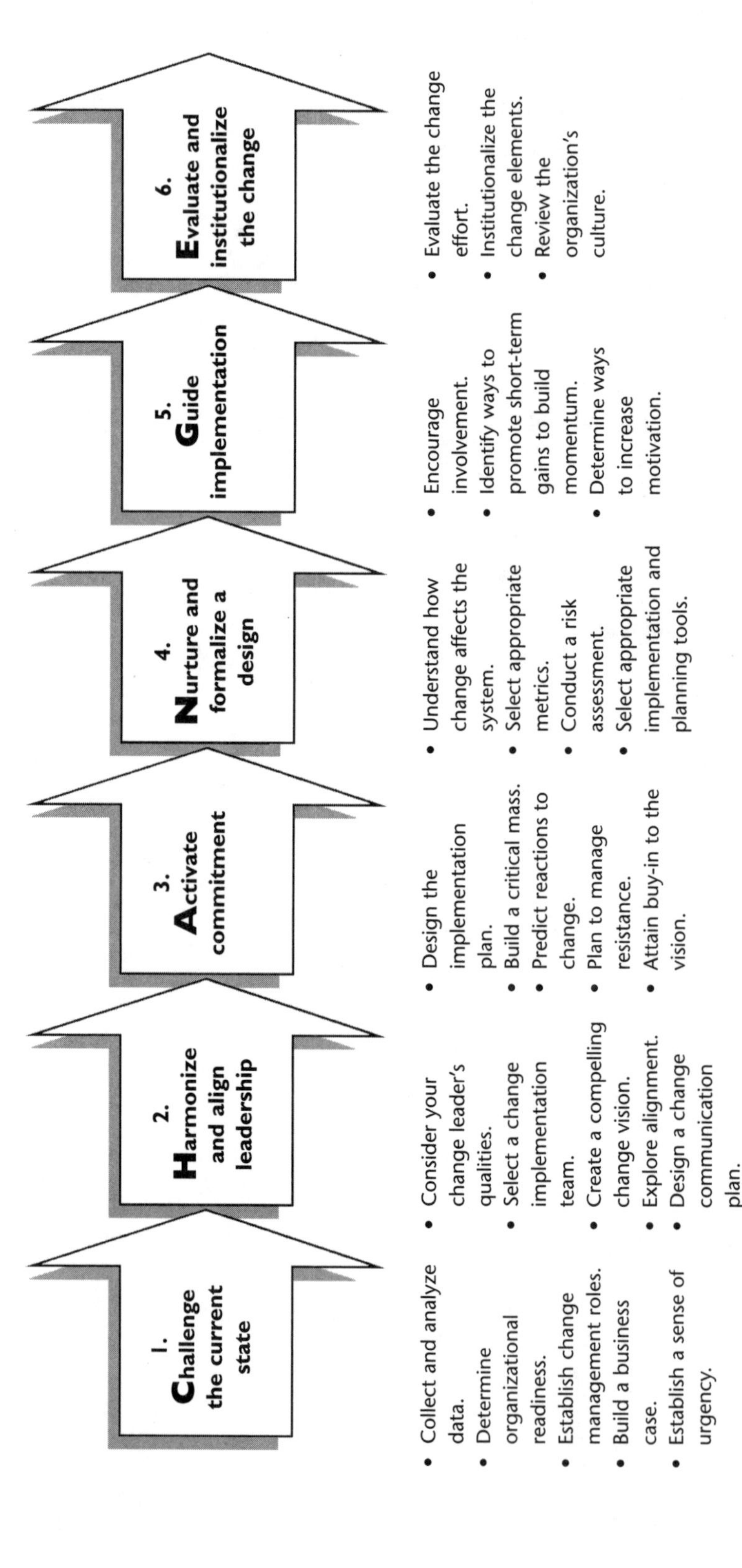

Remember, too, that change does not have a strong record of success. There are many reasons. You will increase your chances of success if you plan for, address, and deliver all the elements discussed in each step. To review the steps, see figure 9-1.

Checklist for Step 6: Evaluate and Institutionalize the Change

- ❑ A monitoring plan has been established.
- ❑ A follow-up plan has been developed to focus on key transition areas.
- ❑ Someone is responsible for ensuring that the change is being monitored.
- ❑ The organization has evaluated the effort against the plan.
- ❑ Contingency plans have been implemented where necessary.
- ❑ The change process has been evaluated.
- ❑ Individuals were involved in the evaluation.
- ❑ The lessons learned have been captured.
- ❑ Best practices have been identified and recorded.
- ❑ Steps have been taken to institutionalize the change.
- ❑ Teams have been closed out appropriately.
- ❑ The teams have celebrated successes.

Part III

Support for Change

Chapter 10

Toward a Perspective on Change: The Big Picture and the Future

Reasonable men adapt to their environment;
unreasonable men try to adapt the environment
to themselves.
—George Bernard Shaw

In prosperity, prepare for a change;
in adversity, hope for one.
—Anonymous

In This Chapter:

- Essential rules for navigating change
- The politics of change
- The future of change: the change-ready organization

This chapter brings together a few topics that we did not cover in the first nine chapters. It begins with a reminder of some important common-sense rules of the road. Implementing a change effort requires leaders and change agents to remember so many things. In some cases, you may be involved in a large-scale change and it may feel as if you are creating an entirely new entity. In other cases, even if the change is smaller, you will still need to remember the same elements of change. Therefore, it is always good to come back to the roots of change—the indispensable words of advice that provide the foundation for a good change initiative.

Politics plays a role in most organizations, and this chapter explores the role it plays in change. I've been witness to a couple of organizational change efforts that have come to a complete standstill or were ended due to an internal political ploy. In one case, the results were good for the organization; in the others, they were not. Unfortunately, the people who suffered the most were the employees. And of course the next time the organizations mentioned future change, the employees responded with, "Yaah right!" or "Here we go again!" leading to a let's-wait-and-see stance by many individuals.

Finally, this chapter addresses the future of change. It is no surprise that change is here to stay. With information doubling every one to two years, a new iPod model on the market every couple of months, and cell phone features multiplying weekly, you can expect your organization to be immersed in a change of one kind or another almost constantly. Creating and staffing the change-ready organization will be imperative to stay in the business game.

Essential Rules for Navigating Change

You've read nine word-filled chapters. Sometimes all you need are a few reminders. If that's the case, this section will suit your needs just fine! It contains a half dozen lists—essential underpinnings of change. I hope these lists provide you with the kind of advice you need when you don't have time to read the whole book, or even a chapter.

Eleven Essentials for Any Change Journey

Your strategy will guide the implementation of significant change. Consider these tactics as underpinnings to ensure that your strategy can be carried out more easily. These 11 guidelines become standard operating procedures for successful change journeys:

1. Create a vision, establish goals, measure the outcome, and provide feedback.
2. Ensure that there is a good rationale for making a change, and readily share the value it will add.
3. Invest the resources required for success.
4. Create teams to plan, coordinate, implement, and troubleshoot the intervention, led by people who are trusted, respected, and recognized for following through.
5. Involve as many people as possible, especially the organization's informal leaders.
6. Provide coaching, mentoring, training, and guidance to ensure that individuals are successful in the new process or in the changed organization.

7. Communicate, communicate, communicate. Listen, listen, listen.
8. Reward and reinforce people, celebrate successes—large and small.
9. Use the power of an external consultant if you need to reinforce the plan, provide additional expertise, or add credibility.
10. Create new signs and symbols, logos, and events to celebrate the change.
11. Align the people and the systems with the new organization.

Four Questions That Every Employee Wants Answered

A number of researchers state that employees have the ability to resist change, create turmoil, and significantly delay change initiatives. Although I don't buy that completely, employees can create a huge financial and productivity drain if not led carefully through the morass of change. All employees want the same things as you and I. Answer these questions and get them involved:

1. "What is happening?"
2. "Why is it happening?"
3. "How will this affect me and my job? WIIFM (What's in it for me)?"
4. "What's the plan for getting there?"

Ten Critical Factors to Maintain the Gain

Institutionalizing the change is critical, yet stories abound that tell of going back to "the way we've always done it." The following suggestions provide the most payoff for your effort. They are indeed basic. But they work. And perhaps that's why you continue to hear them over and over:

1. Plan for institutionalizing the change right from the start.
2. Reward those who are doing it right.
3. Ignore or remove those who are doing it wrong, sabotaging the effort, or just refuse to play by the new rules.
4. Develop a way to ensure that leadership development and succession planning support the vision.
5. Ensure that internal and external training and coaching echo the message.
6. Change policies, procedures, pay and benefit systems, structures, and other guidelines and rules that undermine the change goal.
7. Remove the old ways (equipment, processes, people) so that there is no other way to complete the work.
8. Establish a warning system for regressive behavior.
9. Articulate the relationship between new behaviors and organizational success.
10. Monitor the change and ensure that the reporting mechanism is available to everyone at any time.

Seven Keys to Unleashing Your Influence as a Change Agent

Are you facilitating change for your organization? It's outlandish for me to think (or for you to believe) that a list of a mere seven things could ensure your success as you facilitate the change in your organization. They won't. These seven, however, are things that you would not think of unless you've already been through the process. Although they did not make it anywhere else in the book, consider them a gift from one change agent to another:

1. Tell the emperor or empress when the attire is inappropriate; remember, you may be the only one who has done that in a long time.
2. Select people to be on a team whom you trust; you will waste time worrying about sneaks, snakes, and secretives.
3. Nip it in the bud; no matter what "it" is, it ain't going to go away, so just do whatever you need to do immediately.
4. Ask for help; you can't do it alone; get those high-paid leaders out of their corner offices and out in the cubbies with you. And bring in someone from the outside to help you get started or to bail you out of trouble when it happens.
5. Develop a sense to observe things as they really are, not as they appear to be; ask lots of questions to uncover the truth.
6. Grow a thick hide; you'll receive a fair share of abuse, but it's all a part of getting the job done.
7. Finally, don't count on lists; they always leave something important out!

Five Laws of Change

Change is difficult, demanding, and messy. It is easy to get lost in the mass of theories, strategies, models, and approaches (see chapter 1). After you've read all the books by all the experts in the field, it all boils down to five rules:

1. Change starts at the top.
2. Communication is crucial.
3. People change, not organizations.
4. People choose whether to change.
5. A change effort will be more difficult than you imagined, more costly than you estimated, and take longer than you planned.

The Six Biggest Barriers to Successful Change

As a result of reading almost every book published about change since 1998, and on the basis of a fair share of first-hand experience, I have deduced that these are the big six—the obstacles that will most likely undermine your change effort. Have I listed all of them? Probably not, but these will keep you *really* busy until you uncover the rest!

1. *Corporate culture*—which is why, even though you can't change it instantly, you need to know how to work within it.

2. *A lack of resources*—whether time, money, or people, organizations tend to underestimate the real need.
3. *Limited executive support*—whether in action or visibility, reality or perception, without the execs doing the talking and the walking, the effort will lack the momentum it needs. Major change efforts cannot be delegated down.
4. *Employee resistance*—even though I think the root cause is most often poor planning by the change project designers, a lack of effort to get employees on board and to communicate often and early. I mention it here because so many change gurus list it as a barrier to success.
5. *Poor planning or a lack of planning*—the foundation of any good change effort. Enough said.
6. *A lack of credibility*—partly related to all of the above. So figure out why the change is clashing with the culture; why executives are not out there singing the change song; and why the vision, data, and business case are not compelling. If these things are addressed appropriately, the change effort will attain the credibility it deserves.

Winning Idea:
Check out Rosabeth Moss Kanter's "10 Change Commandments" from her coauthored book *The Challenge of Organizational Change*. It's a good read for a more in-depth examination of organizational change.

The Politics of Change

After that light dose of lists, let's consider a heavier topic: organizational politics, what you need to know, and how you relate it to organizational change. An important part of effective change is understanding the politics that lie just beneath the surface of the organization:

- Who supports whom?
- Who influences whom?
- What fears do individuals have?
- What are they afraid of?
- What are each person's goals?
- Where is each open to negotiation?
- Who can be bought and with what?

Organizations are social entities that struggle for limited resources. Individuals and groups inside organizations execute various tactics to "win" the struggle for money, people, space, and even attention. This contradicts teamwork, undermines collective goals, and suboptimizes the organization.

So how does this affect you? Politics can interfere with normal processes, such as how decisions are made, how rewards are distributed, and who is promoted. And implementing a change effort quickly usurps resources for all the reasons we've discussed in previous chapters. You could easily be giving up resources to organizational politics and not even know it.

In *The Fifth Discipline*, Peter Senge states that it all begins with a shared vision: "Without a genuine sense of common vision and values, there is nothing to motivate people beyond self-interest." Now you understand another reason why a shared common vision is so critical. In *The Empowered Manager*, Peter Block presents the five elements of "enlightened" self-interest, which views politics from a positive perspective as an act of "service, contribution, and creations." Choosing and cultivating Block's five elements (meaning, contribution and service, integrity, positive impact on other people, and mastery) demonstrates the positive side of politics.

Winning Idea: Grab a copy of Peter Block's *The Empowered Manager: Positive Political Skills at Work* to read firsthand about the five elements of enlightened self-interest.

Individuals have choices about whether to use politics from a positive or negative perspective. What can you do as one of the facilitators of change in your organization? The politics will be there—self-interest or enlightened self-interest. So the first step is to understand it, both positive and negative. Who are the movers and shakers? Who has the leader's ear? Who's loyal to whom? Who has little to lose in the hierarchy? Who can you count on to do the right thing for the organization?

The second step is determining how you can use the politics that currently exist to make the change happen. Establish relationships with informal leaders who embody the vision in their words and deeds. Invest time with those who can influence the rest of the organization, thus multiplying your efforts. If you are coaching, introduce the leadership to the concept of positive politics.

Finally, be a model of positive "enlightened" politics for the rest of the organization.

The Future of Change: The Change-Ready Organization

This book begins with the words, "Change—ever present, ever accelerating." Expecting the unexpected is a way of life. It doesn't have to be that way. Today's organizations must build capacity into themselves to tackle the accelerating rate of ongoing change. They must become change-ready organizations.

Becoming a Change-Ready Organization

Becoming a change-ready organization is a topic that needs an entire book to cover all the nuances to analyze, design, and transition. A change-ready organization is one that is able to handle the multiple changes of an unpredictable future that is moving more and more rapidly. In an article for *T+D* (January 2003), Pat McLagan states that "the major effort must go into making the organization more adaptable and flexible so that it can learn as it goes along." But just what does that mean?

Remember Peter Senge's *The Fifth Discipline: The Art and Practice of the Learning Organization*? If you read it in 1990 when it was published, or if you've never read it, it is time to pull it off the bookshelf (every organization that thought it was successful bought at least several copies) and dust it off. It's time to read it—this time with an eye toward what it takes to be adaptable and flexible. Read it with an appreciation for the agile organization required for the future. Read it with an appreciation for the "learning organization."

In *The Fifth Discipline*, Senge defines the learning organization as "an organization that is continually expanding its capacity to create its future." I am not going to reiterate all that Senge says in his book. There is not space to do that, and I am certainly not as eloquent in my writing as he is.

It's clear that if our organizations are to keep up with their demanding change schedules, they will need to be change ready.

Winning Idea:
Find a copy of *The Fifth Discipline* by Peter Senge and read at least chapters 1 through 4. If you aren't hooked by then, the timing may not be right for you. If you read it a decade or two ago, read it again, this time with a new appreciation of the changes that make up the 21st century.

What Is a Change-Ready Organization?

A change-ready organization displays many of the characteristics addressed throughout this book. It embraces these cultural norms:

- Encourages learning
- Rewards creativity and risk taking
- Promotes teamwork and partnering
- Allows failure
- Rewards knowledge sharing
- Engages in ongoing incremental change
- Supports employee involvement at all levels
- Celebrates and embraces change
- Links the present to the future.

How Do You Create a Change-Ready Organization?

Here's the challenge! What we are really talking about is changing the culture—a lengthy process, which by many standards takes at least seven years. And at the end of the seventh year? More change! The transition never ends. In reality, the arbitrary seven-year period never ends. Organizations must continue to reinvent themselves to be ready for change.

The ideas here suggest what you need to do to get started. It should by no means be considered all that you need to do. The ideas are divided into three categories: people, organizational learning, and processes. Although the dividing lines are not perfectly clear between the categories, you'll get the picture.

People:

- Change recruiting practices to identify targeted skills
- Hire employees who embrace the characteristics listed below
- Promote and develop people who can implement the organization's vision
- Grow change-enabling supervisors and managers

- Establish means to listen to, encourage, and reward mavericks and trailblazers
- Build trust throughout the organization.

Organizational learning:

- Make training available to everyone
- Ensure that learning is a daily occurrence
- Educate employees in empowerment, creativity, teamwork, and change
- Learn as an organization
- Capture and utilize lessons learned
- Assign stretch tasks that develop people for future responsibility.

Processes:

- Become future-focused with a compelling vision
- Retool the pay and benefit system to reward those who support, encourage, and lead change
- Remove barriers to change
- Establish a system to share knowledge across boundaries
- Encourage and reward entrepreneurship
- Initiate improvement efforts that enable many employees to be involved
- Implement processes to monitor and measure results
- Identify how to create agile processes that allow the organization to turn on a dime.

What Employee Characteristics Exemplify the Change-Ready Organization?

The employee who is successful in a change-ready organization has skills similar to those in innovative organizations. Characteristics could include some of these:

- lifelong learner
- creative
- high tolerance for ambiguity
- team player
- takes risks without prodding
- learns from mistakes
- shares knowledge and teaches others
- challenges traditional approaches and the status quo
- excellent communicator with an emphasis on listening
- problem solver.

With landmarks like these, leaders may be better equipped in the future to plot a smooth course and a road map for change, avoiding many of the potholes, detours, and other hazards that currently curtail the change journey.

Chapter 11

Activities to Support the CHANGE Journey

This chapter is a toolbox containing activities you can use with the implementation team, the change leader, individuals, and other groups. Some of the activities are self-reflection activities that you may wish to complete as well. The preceding chapters suggest appropriate times within the CHANGE Model to use each activity. However, feel free to use these activities where they make the most sense and where your individual staff members and teams need to use them. The purpose statement at the start of each activity identifies the objective(s) the activity has been designed to achieve. The activities are:

1. Five-Why Technique (Chapter 4)
2. Change Readiness Predictor Discussion (Chapter 4)
3. Change Agents Unite! (Chapter 4)
4. Oh, the Places You'll Go! (Chapter 4)
5. Leader Assessment (Chapter 5)
6. Exploring Barriers (Chapter 5)
7. From Barriers to Box Office Hit (Chapter 5)
8. Team Member Selection (Chapter 5)
9. Resisting Change (Chapter 6)
10. Employees Speak Up (Chapter 6)
11. Force Field Analysis (Chapter 6)
12. Vision Feedback (Chapter 6)
13. Systems: Thinking About Ours (Chapter 7)
14. Pre-Metrics (Chapter 7)
15. Build Trust (Chapter 8)
16. Holding On and Letting Go (Chapter 8)
17. Conversations for a Change (Chapter 8)

18. 101 Ways to Reward Employees (Chapter 8)
19. Six-Pack Retake (Chapter 8)
20. Evaluate for Impact (Chapter 9)
21. Evaluate the Change Process (Chapter 9)
22. Helping Employees Succeed with Change (Appendix B)
23. Lessons Learned for Leaders (Chapter 9).

Each activity is described on the following pages. For those activities that have an accompanying worksheet, the worksheet is given here, as well as on the CD that accompanies this book.

Activity 1. Five-Why Technique (Chapter 4)

Purpose: Ensure you are addressing root causes during data gathering.

Process:

1. You can do this exercise yourself or with a small group (it's more fun that way).
2. Select a symptom or what you think may be the cause of a problem.
3. Ask, "Why is this happening?" List all responses, on paper if you are doing this alone or on a flipchart pad if you are facilitating a group. You may wish to start by listing the initial answers across the paper horizontally to create columns in preparation for the next round of responses.
4. Repeat the question for every response you receive. List the responses close to the word/phrase you are asking about.
5. Continue to repeat the question, "Why is this happening?" until the responses begin to converge to one root cause or until the responses no longer make sense.
6. You will most likely notice duplications and similarities if you follow several of the columns.

Worksheet 11-1. Change Readiness Predictor

Indicate the degree to which each of the dimensions is a concern to you with regard to your organization's change readiness. Circle the number under the appropriate heading for each factor. Dimensions have been scaled according to their relative importance in predicting the receptivity to change. Total the scores for an overall change readiness index.

	Degree of Concern				
Dimension	**No**	**Little**	**Moderate**	**Substantial**	**Critical**
Comprehensive variables:					
Size of change	4	3	2	1	0
Current internal stress	4	3	2	1	0
External impact	4	3	2	1	0
Change history	4	3	2	1	0
Supportive culture	4	3	2	1	0
Clear internal processes	4	3	2	1	0
Resources:					
Access to workforce	8	6	4	2	0
Workforce flexibility/agility	8	6	4	2	0
Unions/other constraints	8	6	4	2	0
Time commitment	8	6	4	2	0
Money available	8	6	4	2	0
Employee considerations:					
Workforce talent	12	9	6	3	0
Executive leadership	12	9	6	3	0
Skilled change agents	12	9	6	3	0
Management support	12	9	6	3	0
Total the scores for all dimensions:					

Total all columns: __________

If the total change readiness score is: less than 50, conduct crisis intervention before beginning; if it is between 50 and 69, proceed with caution, taking all steps in the process to ensure success; if it is greater than 69, the organization is ready for the planned change.

Source: ebb associates inc, 2004.

Activity 2. Change Readiness Predictor Discussion (Chapter 4)

Purposes:

- Identify the organization's readiness for change
- Identify actions required to ensure the effort goes more smoothly.

Process:

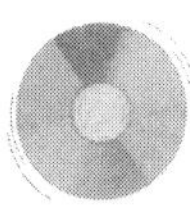

1. Provide a copy of the Change Readiness Predictor (worksheet 11-1) for each person in the group and ask him or her to complete the questions (a reproducible PDF of this worksheet is on the CD accompanying this volume).
2. Questions to open the discussion may include:
   — Which area did you score the lowest?
   — Why do you think that is?
   — What can we do before initiating a change that would make the effort go more smoothly?
   — Which are the least problematic? Why do you suppose that is?
   — How can we leverage the positive areas?
3. If scores are unusually low, the group can explore specific preliminary actions that need to be taken to increase chances for success. For example, if unions or other groups pose a situation that may prevent success, the group might identify ways to begin to work earlier with the unions.
4. Leave with actions that include who will do what by when; and a monitoring plan.

Worksheet 11-2. Change Agents Unite!

Below is a list of effective change agent/facilitator characteristics:

- Credible
- Trusted and respected
- Tolerance for ambiguity
- Self-confident
- Persistent
- Ability to influence
- Attentive listener
- Eager for improvement
- Process oriented
- Customer focused
- Organizational knowledge
- Big picture vision
- Detail orientation
- People person
- Passion
- Deals well with negativity
- Creative idea-person
- Collaborator
- Achievement oriented
- Realistic
- Sense of timing
- Interest in change
- Logical thinker
- Excellent communicator

1. Identify the five characteristics that you think are your strongest and highlight them with a green marker.

2. Identify the five characteristics that you think you may need support with and highlight them with an orange marker.

3. Find someone who has selected a strength where you marked needed support or vice versa (you marked it as a strength and someone else needs support in that area). Discuss:
   - — Why is it a strength for one of you?
   - — Why is it not a strength for the other?
   - — How important do you believe this particular characteristic is for the task of being a change agent?
   - — How can you help each other?

Activity 3. Change Agents Unite! (Chapter 4)

Purpose: Explore the role of the change agent.

Process:

1. Gather the individuals together who will serve as change agents either full time or as an assigned collateral duty.
2. Provide each of them with the handout for this activity, worksheet 11-2 (also available on the CD accompanying this volume). Give them each a green and an orange highlighter. Tell them to follow the instructions, marking their top five strengths with the green highlighter and marking the five in which they may need additional support with the orange highlighter.

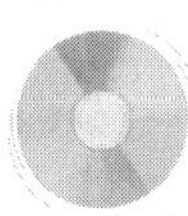

3. Tell them to stand up and locate someone who has selected a strength (green) that matches one they marked that needed support (orange) or vice versa, and to discuss the questions. Give them about five to seven minutes for the discussion:
   - Why is it a strength for one of you?
   - Why is it not a strength for the other?
   - How important do you believe this characteristic is for being a change agent?
   - How can you help each other?
4. Call time and have them each identify the five strengths that they believe are the most important in this organization for success as a change agent. Have them circle the five that are most important.
5. Post the list of strengths on a flipchart at the front of the room. Go through each one and ask them to raise their hands if they think it is a required characteristic for success. Post the number of votes on the left side of the chart. Next go through the list, asking them to raise their hands if they marked it as one of their strengths. Post the numbers on the right side.
6. Lead a discussion, using these questions:
   - What do these numbers tell us?
   - How can we leverage the strengths in the group?
   - Which areas do we need to improve the most?
   - How can we improve the areas that need improving?
   - What are the next steps for this group?

Variation: This activity works best with at least 10 people. If you have fewer than 10, you may want to work through step 3 as a large group instead of in pairs.

Worksheet 11-3. Oh, the Places You'll Go!

Make your personal commitment to conducting the best darn change efforts in the world. In the Dr. Seuss book *Oh, the Places You'll Go!* characters react and respond to change differently:

- The path to change can be either pleasurable or miserable.
- The road to change may be a daunting experience or an exhilarating one.
- The experience can be one that you hope will go away or one that evokes responsibility to get it done.
- Change can be an exciting open road or a speed bump to avoid.

1. How did you feel when you were asked to sit in a circle to read the Dr. Seuss book?

____

2. How helpful is this reaction to change? ______________________

3. What reactions do you anticipate from individuals in your organization? How can you address them?

____

____

____

4. In your role as a change agent, identify three things you will do to help us navigate through change.

- ____
- ____
- ____

5. What skills will you need for this task?

____

____

____

Activity 4. Oh, the Places You'll Go! (Chapter 4)

This activity was inspired by one used by Suzanne Schmidt and Joanne Sujansky in their book *Training Games for Managing Change* (1999).

Purposes:

- Prepare change agents for their roles
- Discuss the kinds of reactions that people have toward change.

Process:

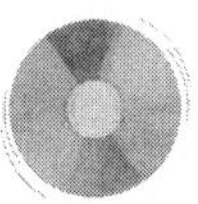

1. Prepare by making copies of worksheet 11-3 for each participant (also available on companion CD). You will also need two copies of the book *Oh, the Places You'll Go!* by Dr. Seuss.
2. Have all the participants gather in a large circle. While sitting in the circle, begin to read the first page or two of the book. Pass the book to the person sitting next to you and have that person read a page or two.
3. As each participant reads from one book and passes it around, you will hold the second book open facing the participants so that they can see the pictures. Continue around the room until the book is complete.
4. Pass out worksheet 11-3 and ask the participants to complete the questions.
5. When finished, process the activity by asking these questions:
   — How did you initially feel about sitting in a circle to read a Dr. Seuss book?
   — What does that tell you about reactions to change?
   — What might others, especially those who resist change, feel about this activity? How can you translate that back to the workplace?
   — What reactions do you expect to encounter regarding this change effort?
   — What skills will you need to polish in preparation for your role as a change agent?
   — What thoughts has this activity stimulated for you?
6. Say, "I'd like to leave you with one lasting thought, and that is that, like the Dr. Seuss book, everyone sees change differently. I hope that each of you sees the possibilities in change and appreciates all the places that being a good facilitator of change will take you. . . . All the opportunities. . . . All the exciting future possibilities. . . .
   "Oh, the Places You'll Go!"

Worksheet 11-4. Leader VIEW Assessment

Complete the following self-assessment. Then schedule a time to discuss it with your change facilitator.

Characteristic	Yes	No	Not Sure
Visionary			
• Ability to imagine the future			
• Focuses on results			
• Articulate; excellent communicator			
• Strategic thinker			
• Challenges the status quo			
• Comfortable with ambiguity			
• Willing to take calculated risks			
• Anticipates the unexpected			
Inspiring			
• Sells the vision, benefits, and what can be			
• Genuine; models the intended change			
• Passionate; evokes followers to get on board			
• Engaging; builds alliances across the organization			
• Trusts others, and is trusted			
• Aware of how own behavior has an impact on others			
• Comfortable making presentations in public			
• Remains calm during turmoil			
Enthusiastic			
• Energizes others to overcome barriers			
• Involves others; collaborative			
• Open to others' ideas; allows for mistakes			
• Rewards and appreciates others			
• Able to use humor to relieve tense situations			
• Caring; empathizes with others			
• Maintains positive, focused attitude			
• Persistent despite obstacles			
Wise			
• Has wisdom in many areas			
• Knowledgeable of organizations, people, and processes			
• Analytical; understands data and can develop solutions			
• Anticipates and addresses issues			
• Exudes business acumen			
• Is a problem solver			
• Is politically astute			
• Knows how to obtain resources			

Activity 5. Leader Assessment (Chapter 5)

Purpose: Assess the leader's skills.

Process:

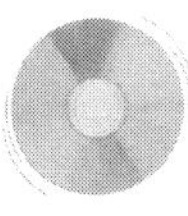

1. Ask the leader to complete the self-assessment, worksheet 11-4 (also available on companion CD).
2. Schedule a time to discuss the assessment with the leader, using these questions:
   — What are your strengths?
   — What are the areas that need the most work?
   — How can you use your strengths to make other improvements?
   — How can I help you?
3. Plan a follow-up meeting.

Worksheet 11-5. Exploring Barriers

Barrier	Root Cause	Approach
Lack of a clear vision		
Insufficient information		
Limited management support		
Lack of communication		
Organizational complacency		
Lack of change leadership experience		
Lack of planning for resistance		
Lack of time		
Insufficient resources allocated		
Policies not aligned to the change		
Poor follow-through		
Lack of rewards for change or consequences for not changing		

Activity 6. Exploring Barriers (Chapter 5)

Purposes:

- Provide an opportunity for the implementation team to consider potential barriers and how to address them before they arise
- Opportunity for the implementation team to practice team problem solving before an actual problem arises.

Process:

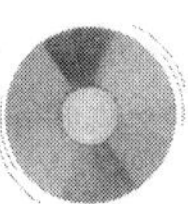

1. Invite the implementation team to explore potential barriers so that they can be prepared for the future. Make copies of worksheet 11-5 and hand them out to the team members (available on the CD accompanying this volume).
2. Work through the first barrier as a large group, identifying the cause and the strategy the team would implement. Split the team in half and assign each group five of the barriers.
3. Allow about 15 minutes for them to complete the task. Then get together as an entire group to discuss the responses and ways of overcoming the barriers.
4. Wrap up by asking the team the likelihood of any of these barriers becoming a reality. Finally, ask if there is anything that should be put in place immediately.

Activity 7. From Barriers to Box Office Hit (Chapter 5)

Purposes:

- Provide an opportunity to explore barriers to successful change
- Identify ways to increase the chances of a successful change effort.

Process:

1. Ask participants to think of a time when they went through a successful change. What made it successful? Post their responses on a flipchart.
2. Ask participants to think of a time when they went through a difficult change. What made it difficult? Post their responses.
3. Ask what commonalities exist between the two lists? Circle them.
4. Ask people to move into smaller groups (depending upon the number of categories you wish to explore).
5. Say, "Looking at this list, what can we do to ensure a 'Box office hit'? Like the Oscars, we have categories in which to identify the winners. May I have the envelope, please!" Hand out a sealed envelope to each small group. Inside each envelope is one category written on a piece of paper. Suggested categories include employees, transitions, leadership, resources, commitment, implementation, communication, culture, systems, and others that are important to your organization. Allow about 10 minutes for them to identify as many things as possible to support a successful change effort. Ask them to write the ideas legibly on the page that was inside their envelope.
6. Ask for each group to report its best idea. Allow for some discussion about the ideas.
7. Gather the pages of ideas. Thank them and tell them that they will see their ideas manifest themselves in the implementation plan.

Variation:

- In keeping with the box office hit theme, hang old movie posters in the room and serve popcorn.
- If you have time, you can have each subgroup read its entire list and you could post the ideas on a flipchart.

Worksheet 11-6. Decision Matrix for Selecting Team Members

Assign a letter from A to F, and so on, to each person you are considering. Use the following rating scale: 1 = never; 2 = rarely; 3 = sometimes; 4 = usually; 5 = always.

Criterion	A	B	C	D	E	F
Select the right people:						
• Offers executive-level support						
• Is an informal leader						
• Possesses required expertise and knowledge						
• Is credible throughout the organization						
• Capable leader and manager						
• Respected and trusted by other executives						
From the right areas:						
• Fulfills cross-section representation						
• Respected by all stakeholders						
• Represents the most critical area						
• Ability to allocate resources						
With the right attitude:						
• Positive						
• Trusting						
• Problem solver						
• Enthusiastic						
• Persistent						
• Team player						

Activity 8. Team Member Selection (Chapter 5)

Purpose: Use criteria to select team members.

Process:

1. Bring a few leaders together to select members for the implementation team.
2. Use the decision matrix, worksheet 11-6 (also available on companion CD). Assign a letter to each person you are considering for the team.
3. You may wish to add or change the criteria as identified.
4. Have each person complete the matrix and use it to contribute to the discussion.
5. Lead a discussion in which you reach consensus about the individuals.

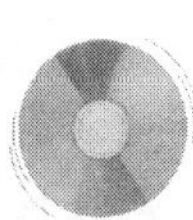

Variation: The tool is equally successful when used by one person to make a decision.

Worksheet 11-7. Spiral of Change

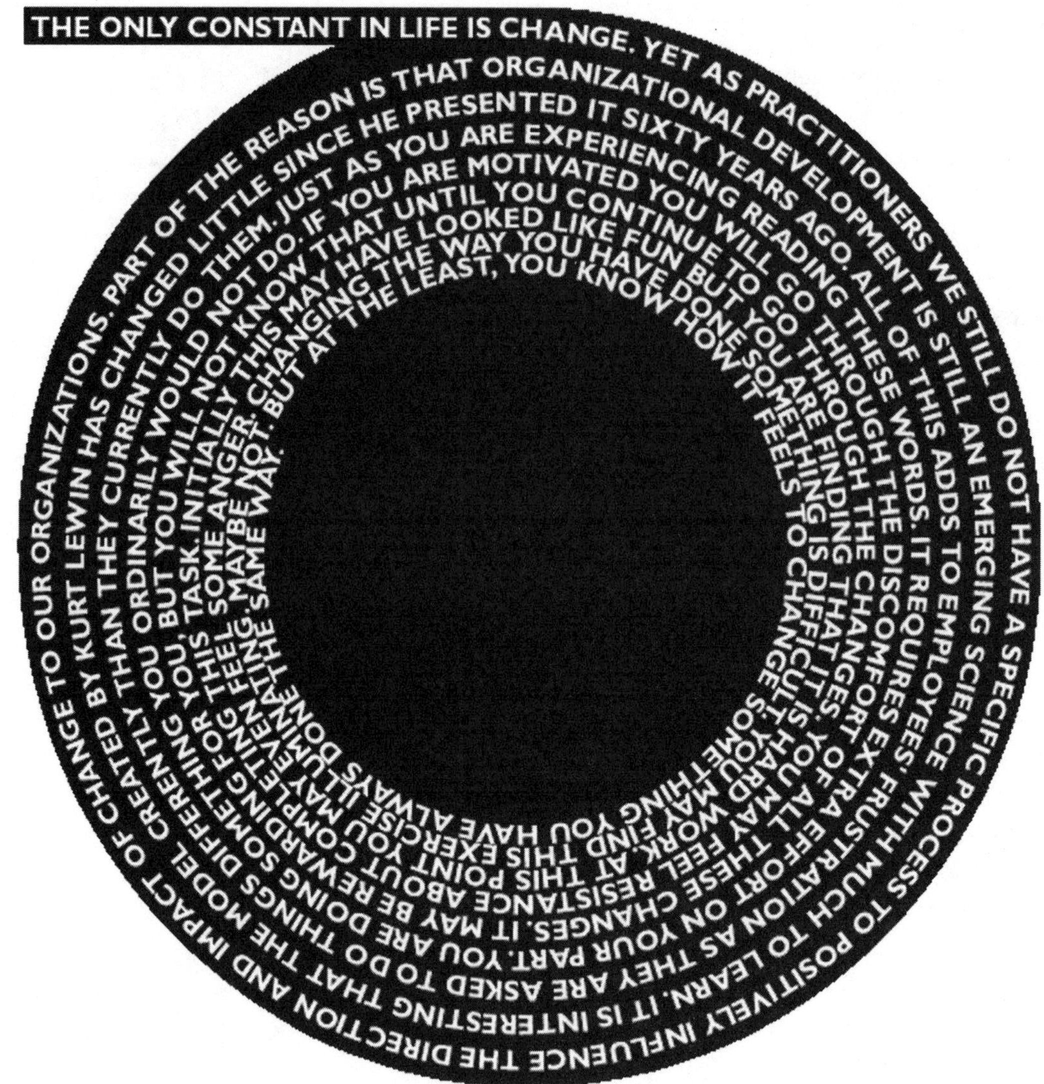

Source: ebb associates inc.

Activity 9. Resisting Change (Chapter 6)

Purpose: Experience on a small scale some of the feelings of resistance to change.

Process:

1. Give a copy of the Spiral of Change (worksheet 11-7) to everyone (also available on the CD accompanying this volume). Tell them to read the message without giving any further instructions.
2. Once everyone has completed (or has given up) reading the Spiral of Change, ask these questions:
   — How did you feel when you started this exercise?
   — How did your feelings change over time?
   — Why did that happen?
   — If you gave up and quit, why?
   — If you made it to the end, was it worth the effort? Why?
   — How is this exercise related to change?
3. Explain that they have just experienced resistance to change on a very small scale. You may wish to make some of these points if they do not come up in the discussion:
   — You probably felt excited when you started the exercise and became bored or maybe even irritated as the message continued on and on.
   — If you reached the end, you probably were a bit disappointed because the end does not reveal anything very exciting except that you have completed the task.
   — Some perhaps gave up and quit because you thought you had better ways to spend your time.
   — And throughout the experience, you could see no good reason how reading in a spiral was any better than the "way you've always done it before," left to right!
4. Conclude with these questions:
   — What did you learn about change based on this exercise?
   — What are the lessons learned that we should take forward?

Worksheet 11-8. Employees Speak Up

Why does change seem to be uncomfortable and threatening?

Change expert William Bridges, author of *Managing Transitions,* says that employees expect these four Ps to be more accepting of change:

- Purpose or the reasons for the change.
- Picture of the expected outcome.
- Plan for navigating from the current situation to the future.
- Part the employee will play in making the changes successful.

Take a minute to think about the last time you resisted change.

What changes have you resisted in the past? ______________________________

____

____

Why did you resist change? ______________________________

____

____

What strategies would have reduced your resistance? Do any of these strategies match Bridges's four Ps?

____

____

Think about the current change effort our organization is implementing. What recommendations do you have for management to make the change more acceptable to employees?

____

____

Activity 10. Employees Speak Up (Chapter 6)

Purpose: Provide an opportunity for employees to give feedback anonymously to their managers about a current change effort.

Process:

1. Begin by asking the group, "Why do so many employees find change to be uncomfortable and threatening?" If you have a large group, post responses on a flipchart.
2. Explain that the change expert William Bridges, the author of *Managing Transitions*, says that leaders will be more successful if they provide the workforce with these four Ps when introducing change:
   — Purpose or the reasons for the change.
   — Picture of the expected outcome.
   — Plan for navigating from the current situation to the future.
   — Part the employee will play in making the changes successful.
3. Tell them that they have an opportunity to give feedback to management about the current change effort.
4. Give each participant the Employees Speak Up handout, worksheet 11-8, and allow 10 minutes to complete the questions (also available on companion CD).

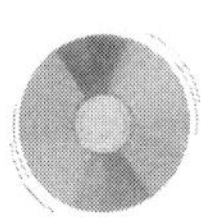

5. Lead a discussion about the group's comments.
6. Conclude by asking what managers may need to do differently to ensure the success of this effort, and post the responses. Ask what the participants may need to do differently to ensure success, and post their responses.
7. Share responses anonymously with the implementation team.

Worksheet 11-9. Force Field Analysis Practice

Think of a personal situation you would like to see changed. Enter the goal or target at the top of the force field analysis diagram below. List all the forces that are working to prevent the change you desire on the right side. List all the forces that work in favor of the change you desire on the left side.

Name the objective, target, need, or goal: ____________________

Better → **Situation** ← **Worse**

Driving forces	**Restraining forces**
→	←
→	←
→	←
→	←
→	←
→	←
→	←
→	←
→	←
→	←
→	←
Forces favoring the change	**Forces resisting the change**

Identify how you can make the driving forces stronger: ____________________

____

____

Identify how you can weaken or eliminate the restraining forces: ____________________

____

____

Activity 11. Force Field Analysis (Chapter 6)

Purpose: Practice using a tool for changing resistance to acceptance.

Process:

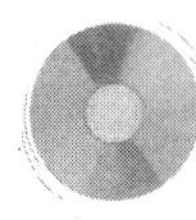

1. Provide each person with two copies of the force field analysis practice page, worksheet 11-9 (also available on CD accompanying this volume).
2. Explain the design and purpose of force field analysis. Explain that the tool was created by Kurt Lewin, who viewed situations as being affected by "a sea of forces in motion." Tell them that some of these forces are positive and desirable, while others are negative and undesirable. These forces are in constant motion and produce stability or, in Lewin's words, "quasi-stationary equilibrium." Force field analysis is a useful concept to help identify the forces at work to produce stability or the status quo.
3. Explain the diagram and suggest that they think of the center line as the status quo—or the way the situation exists today. Various forces have an impact on the status quo (shown by the center line) pushing from opposite sides to hold it firmly in place. Tell them to imagine that the driving forces (the left-hand column) are favorable to the intended change and that the restraining forces (the right-hand column) are those that prevent change. The key is to identify both kinds of forces and then to strengthen the driving forces and weaken the restraining forces.
4. Ask "What is the goal? Which direction do you want the center line to move?" The line should move to the right because it means that the driving forces are stronger than the restraining forces and you are getting closer to your goal.
5. Use a flipchart and post an example if the group is unfamiliar with the tool. Write "Clean out the garage" on the objective line. Fill in the right-hand column first and ask for suggestions, saying "What might be preventing (restraining) you from cleaning out the garage?" Expect things such as "No time," "Don't know what to do with everything," and "Currently know where to find everything." Write these suggestions—one per line—in the right-hand column.
6. Next ask for suggestions for the left hand column, "What could be the driving forces that would encourage you to clean the garage?" Expect things such as "My spouse would be happy," "We could have a party in the garage," "I'd feel a sense of accomplishment," and "I might find things that have been lost." Write these suggestions—one per line—in the left-hand column.
7. Next, move to the bottom of the page and ask "How can we strengthen the driving (left-hand column) forces?" Note these at the bottom of the flipchart.
8. Ask "How can we weaken or eliminate the restraining (right-hand column) forces?" Note these at the bottom of the flipchart.

9. Point out that if the driving forces can be strengthened and the restraining forces can be weakened, the center line (situation) moves toward the right—that is, toward the goal.
10. Ask them to think of a personal need—something they would like to change. Make suggestions, such as organize a closet, lose weight, return to school, start a regular savings plan, take a trip to another country. Allow five minutes for them to complete the first practice page. Ask what they learned during this warm-up.
11. Now ask them to think about the change the organization is attempting. Have them complete the second copy of the force field analysis, worksheet 11-9. Allow 10 minutes for this step.
12. Process the activity with the following questions:
    — What are some of the restraining forces?
    — What are some of the driving forces?
    — What can you do to weaken the restraining forces?
    — What can you do to strengthen the driving forces?
    — What do you think you can do to get to the goal?
    — What will you do as a result of this exercise?
    — What can I do to help you?

Activity 12. Vision Feedback (Chapter 6)

Purposes:

- Provide an opportunity for supervisors to obtain feedback about the vision from their staff
- To begin the buy-in process.

Process:

1. Gather together the people who report directly to you. Post the current version of your organization's vision statement on a flipchart pad, or provide a copy of the vision on paper to each person.
2. Read the vision statement and provide any background information you can. Explain that a vision is much more than just words on a piece of paper; a vision should paint a picture of a desired future state. Let them know that reaching a shared vision is important to the organization.
3. Ask your employees the following questions, and capture their comments for the implementation team (or other appropriate leaders):
   — What does this vision statement say to you?
   — How will your job be different once the vision is achieved? Is this better or not?
   — What is your role in achieving the vision?
   — What do you need (training, skills, resources) to be able to help achieve the vision?
   — How would you improve the vision statement?
   — What will you do differently as a result of this discussion?

Activity 13. Systems: Thinking About Ours (Chapter 7)

Purpose: Explore aspects of the organizational system to ensure that employees support the change.

Process:

1. Ask the group, "What exists in our organization's system that we need to examine to ensure that it is aligned with the change?" Anticipate some of the following:
   — Processes, both primary and related secondary ones that need to change
   — Procedures that are a part of the processes that changed and the standard operating procedures that support them
   — Pay and benefit systems
   — Recognition efforts to support the new design
   — Selection and hiring efforts to bring on people with required competencies
   — Information technology systems that support the change either directly or peripherally
   — New employee orientation and other training efforts
   — Support to supervisors and managers because they hold the organization together during times of change
   — Recruiting methods for the new, changed skill set
   — Budgets, individual development plans, customer expectations, workload, and many others.
2. Ask the group, "How can we find out whether we need to address these items?"
3. Wrap up the discussion by asking "Where do we go from here? What should we do next?

Activity 14. Pre-Metrics (Chapter 7)

Purpose: Refine and review the metrics of the change effort.

Process:

1. This activity is probably best presented to the implementation team. Tell them that they should come prepared to discuss metrics and how they can be used to enable the change effort.
2. Lead the discussion around these eight questions and have someone available to take good notes:
   — What is the most important aspect of metrics that we need to remember as related to our preferred vision?
   — What is the specific purpose of the metric system?
   — How will the measures need to be used? By whom?
   — What behaviors will the metrics reinforce? What processes?
   — What performance will the metrics be tied to?
   — How will data be collected? Analyzed?
   — How will the data be delivered? To whom?
   — How are the data linked to the reward system?
3. On the basis of our discussion, what are the most important metrics for this initiative?
4. Following the meeting, compile the notes and return them to the participants in less than 24 hours. Add your conclusions and recommendations.
5. Meet with each individual to initiate a brief discussion about what needs to be done next.

Variation: Before the meeting, have them read chapter 8 in Jeff Evans and Chuck Schaefer's *Ten Tasks of Change: Demystifying Changing Organizations* (2001).

Worksheet 11-10. Self-Examination for Building Trust

There are four general ways to build and strengthen trust. Number the behaviors from 1 to 4 in order of what you believe is easiest for you; 1 should be easiest and 4 most difficult.

_______ *Honesty and candor.* "I say what I mean." "You will always know where I stand." "You can be straight with me."

_______ *Accessibility and openness.* "I'll tell you all about me." "Tell me what works for you." "Let's keep our agendas open and have fun."

_______ *Approving and accepting.* "I value people and diverse perspectives." "You can count on being heard without judgment or criticism."

_______ *Dependability and trustworthiness.* "I do what I say I will do." "I keep my promises." "You can count on me."

What makes some easier than others for you?

What makes some more difficult for you?

Recognize that what you perceive as easier are the strengths that are natural to you. They are the natural ways you go about building trust with others. Those you listed as more difficult are important to others who do not have the same characteristics as you. Those are the ones you will need to work to improve.

Generally, it is easier to build trust with others who appreciate the same values in building trust that you do. During the change initiative, however, you will work with people who value trust from all perspectives.

Trust will occur more easily if you identify what is important to each individual and focus on what that person needs from you to be able to build trust. You will be more successful building trust with everyone if you can determine what is important to others and focus on those behaviors.

What specific behaviors will you need to practice?

Activity 15. Build Trust (Chapter 8)

Purposes:

- Explore various ways to build trust
- Identify what is natural and what is difficult in building trust with others.

Process:

1. Provide the Building Trust handout, worksheet 11-10, to each participant (also available on the CD accompanying this volume).

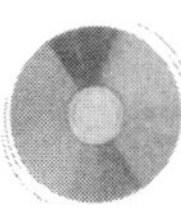

2. Review the four ways to build trust. Tell participants to number the behaviors from 1 to 4 in order of what they believe is easiest for them; 1 should be easiest and 4 most difficult. Tell them to also note what makes some easier and others more difficult in the space available.
3. Tell them that what each of us perceive as our strengths are behaviors that are more natural because of who we are. They are the natural ways you go about building trust with others. Those you listed as more difficult are important to others who do not have the same characteristics as you. Those are the ones you will need to work to improve.
4. Tell them that what's natural for one person is unnatural for another who has an opposite style. In fact, it may even be perceived as negative. For example, someone who builds trust by being "approving and accepting" may perceive someone whose strength is "honesty and candor" as being a know-it-all or insensitive. And the person who builds trust by being "honest and candid" may perceive someone whose strength is "approving and accepting" as soft selling or hiding something. It may seem unusual, but what may appear to be a strength toward building trust by some can seem negative to others.
5. Tell them that the other opposites are "accessibility and openness" and "dependability and trustworthiness." Ask why these two strengths might clash.
6. Tell them that generally it is easier to build trust with others who have the same natural strengths for building trust that you do. However, since they will work with people who value trust from all perspectives, it would be helpful to explore what they can do to improve the most difficult trust builder for each of them.
7. Have them answer the final question on their pages. Remind them of the quotes that follow each of the trust builders.
8. Wrap up by asking participants to suggest trust-building behaviors that they need to improve.

Worksheet 11-11. Holding On and Letting Go

Issue: ______________________________

	Holding On	Letting Go
Advantages		
Disadvantages		

Activity 16. Holding On and Letting Go (Chapter 8)

Purposes:

- Help employees explore personal difficulties of the change initiative
- Identify other ways to look at an issue
- Make decisions about the issue they are holding on to.

Process:

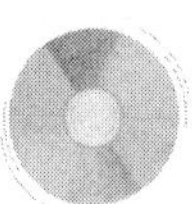

1. Provide each person with a copy of the Holding On and Letting Go handout, worksheet 11-11 (also available on companion CD). Have them identify the issue in their own words. For example:
   — My manager did not tell me about the move.
   — The Milwaukee Division should not have closed.
   — I don't like the new software we are required to use.
   — They should not have dismantled our team.
2. Ask them to quickly complete the grid, filling in as many advantages and disadvantages as they can in all four quadrants. Tell them that single words and phrases are OK as long as they make sense. Tell them that there will be a prize for those who can fill in the most answers in five minutes. Look at your watch to make it appear that you are timing them to the second. Say "Ready, set, go."
3. Call, "Time!" and ask them to count their responses in each square. Tell them they all had a large number, and share a bag of wrapped candy among everyone.
4. Use a round robin to hear some of their responses. Have them share their responses in the following order, doing all of one quadrant first then moving on to the next:
   — Advantages of holding on
   — Disadvantages of letting go
   (Pause and ask how they are feeling.)
   — Disadvantages of holding on
   — Advantages of letting go
   (Again, pause and ask how they are feeling.)
5. Allow discussion to go on as long as it is productive. People should be coming around to the fact that it is not worthwhile to hold on to the issue. Take care that the discussion doesn't go too long and bog people down. As participants are discussing their thoughts, ask these questions:
   — Is there a way in which you could minimize the positive reasons for holding on?
   — Is there a way in which you could strengthen the advantages for letting go?

6. Summarize with these questions:
   — What was the best part of this exercise?
   — What was the most difficult?
   — What did you learn from this exercise?
   — What are you taking away?
   — What will you do differently as a result?

Variation: This exercise assumes that everyone is addressing the same issue. If not, you may adjust the process by putting participants in small groups or just planning to spend more time on the exercise.

Activity 17. Conversations for a Change (Chapter 8)

Purpose: Provide suggestions for conversation starters that change agents and leaders can use to turn pessimism into positive motivation.

Process:

1. Note that it isn't unusual for pessimism to occur during the implementation stage. It may not be avoidable. However, by redirecting the negative energy, a change facilitator can turn the pessimism into positive motivation.
2. As a change facilitator, you may wish to share these ideas with members of the implementation team, leaders of the change effort, or other change agents.
3. Here are a few ideas to use in beginning these conversations with others:
   — Discuss how change will help individuals personally; listen to their content, but also to their intent. Does their tone of voice give you any clues?
   — Use a "What's good about it?" scenario. Ask individuals to imagine that the change goes as planned, and even if they currently think it is worthless, what might then be good about it. You may need to ask several times, but they will generally find something positive.
   — Release any energy that might be blocking individuals' motivation by asking them to complete sentences such as, "I am afraid the change effort will . . ." or "This change will only be successful if . . ."
   — Use creativity techniques, such as asking them to view the change from the customer's perspective or to view the change 10 years from now. What do they see looking at it from another perspective?
   — You may also wish to implement the SHIFT model that was introduced in chapter 6 during the discussion of resistance to change.

Activity 18. 101 Ways to Reward Employees (Chapter 8)

Purpose: Identify ways to reward employees who are helping with the change initiative.

Process:

1. Begin by introducing the topic with this "lecturette":

    Recognition for a job well done is a top motivator for employee performance. Many immediately translate this to forms of recognition that increase employees' paychecks—raises and promotions. Yet employees are more often motivated by personal, thoughtful recognition that shows true appreciation for a job well done—unique recognition "over and above" the norm of the workplace.

    Cash awards have the advantages of being easy to administer, understood by all, and desirable. The drawbacks of using only cash awards, however, are that there is no lasting value (that is, "no trophy effect"), they are not exotic, they lack creativity and personalization, they can't be enhanced, and they tend to become an "expected" award.

    Research by Dr. Gerald Graham, a professor of management at Wichita State University, found that the most powerful motivator was personalized, instant recognition from employees' managers. His study identified the top five motivating techniques managers could provide:

    — Personal congratulations.
    — A personal note about good performance.
    — Promotions based on performance.
    — Public recognition for good performance.
    — Events to celebrate successes.

2. What can you do to recognize employees in creative, personalized ways? How can you thank others in your department and in other departments for going the extra mile? Let's identify recognition ideas under each of these five categories.
3. Divide the group into five small teams and assign each one of the five motivating techniques. Give each team a flipchart page and a marker. Challenge them to identify as many specific ideas as they can within their category. (Yes, number three may be more difficult with fewer "creative" ideas, but it could include things such as a rotational assignment to another department.) Allow five to 10 minutes.
4. Have each team list their ideas.
5. Ask the group to make a decision about things that could be initiated at this stage of the change effort.
6. Wrap up with each person declaring one thing he or she will do to enhance the motivation that person now uses with his or her change teams or individuals who are promoting change.

Worksheet 11-12. Question Six-Pack

Think of a recent situation that you wish you had handled differently. Respond to these questions.

1. Why are you disappointed in this situation?

2. What negative impact did it have?

3. What do you wish you had done?

4. What can you do to mitigate it now?

5. What do you want to do differently in the future?

6. How will you remember?

Activity 19. Six-Pack Retake (Chapter 8)

Purposes:

- Gain appreciation for better communication during difficult situations
- Identify actions for future improvement.

Process:

1. Use this activity with a change implementation team in the wake of a difficult situation or in preparation for a difficult situation.
2. Say "There will be times during the change effort when you will leave a situation wishing you had handled it differently. It might be that you allowed your irritation to show while answering a question during a meeting. You may have come across as pushing too hard."
3. Note that understanding how we have responded in the past can be a lesson to how we can change for future events.
4. Give participants a copy of the Question Six-Pack (worksheet 11-12), and tell them to think of a specific situation that they wished they had managed differently in the past (also available on the CD accompanying this volume). Give them 10 minutes to complete the questions.

5. Review the questions in order with participants. Do not force participants to respond if they appear reluctant, since their situation might be too embarrassing for them to discuss in front of their peers.
6. End the activity by posting all the ways that people will remember (question 6 of the worksheet) to respond differently in the future. Note that this is the most difficult part. We may know that we want to respond differently but not remember when the time comes.

Variation: If you are the change facilitator, you may wish to use this as a coaching tool with a leader.

Worksheet 11-13. Evaluate for Impact

Change Intervention Goals	Successful? Why or Why Not?	Contingency Steps

Activity 20. Evaluate for Impact (Chapter 9)

Purposes:

- Determine whether the change effort achieved its goals
- Identify the contingency steps involved if all goals have not yet been reached.

Process:

1. Gather the individuals together who were involved in facilitating the change. If more than 20 people were involved, you may wish to hold more than one session.
2. Distribute a copy of the Evaluate for Impact form to everyone (worksheet 11-13; available on companion CD).
3. Have flipchart pages prepared and hanging on the walls around the room. Print one goal per flipchart at the top. (Note: if you have a large number of goals for the effort, use only the top level goals.) Under each goal create a T-grid with "successful" on one side and "not successful" on the other side.
4. Divide participants into subgroups of three to five people. Ask them to go around to each chart and to make a decision about whether the organization reached the goal successfully. Once they decide, tell them to write the reason why they believe it was successful or not on the appropriate side of the T. You should allow about 5 minutes per goal. Give a time warning about half way through this step.
5. Bring everyone back together in the large group. Address the successful goals first. Address any stray comments on the "not successful" side.
6. Address the "not successful" goals. For each one identify a list of steps that need to occur next—contingency plans. Start a new flipchart page for each one that may not be straightforward. In some cases the goals may have been overcome by events and are no longer goals to be reached. If that is the case do not spend time on them.
7. For goals that still need to be completed, ask the group who they believe needs to champion each goal.
8. Use this input to design the contingency plan to share with senior management.

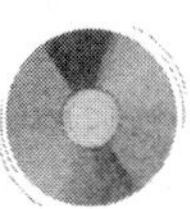

Variation: If this is a very large change effort, you may wish to have different groups address different goals depending upon their roles in the organization. Be sure to include all the goals when you compile the report. Distribute it to everyone.

Worksheet 11-14. Customize Lessons-Learned Evaluation

Event or Action	Failed Miserably	Somewhat Successful	Completely Successful

Activity 21. Evaluate the Change Process (Chapter 9)

Purposes:

- Evaluate the change process
- Identify lessons learned for the next change effort.

Process:

1. Decide whether you will design a tailored evaluation using the format pictured in worksheet 11-14 or if you will use the evaluation format in worksheet 11-15 (both available on the CD accompanying this volume). Make enough copies for those people who will attend.
2. Explain that this evaluation is not about the success of the project—that is, whether we met our goals. Instead, it is about *how* we addressed the change initiative—the process.
3. Distribute the evaluation, worksheet 11-14, to everyone. State that this checklist will serve as a general review of the change intervention and will guide the discussion. State that it will help to generate lessons learned for the organization.
4. Ask them to quietly rate the actions using the broad scale at the top.
5. Once everyone has finished go through the list of actions asking if it was
   - — completely successful?
   - — somewhat successful?
   - — something that failed miserably?
6. Allow discussion of each process. At the end of each process ask:
   - — What successful strategies did we use that we should repeat next time?
   - — What could we do differently/better next time?
   - — How would we change those things? Be specific.
   - — What do we need to start doing that we did not do during this change effort?
   - — What do we consider to be our "best practices" to repeat next time?
7. Give each person an index card and have him or her list two or three lessons learned from this experience. Ask for a few examples.
8. Collect the cards and compile notes from this meeting to share with the leadership.

Variation: If time is limited ask for a couple of examples of successes and then spend the time on those that need the most improvement.

Worksheet 11-15. Evaluate the Change

Event or Action	Failed Miserably	Somewhat Successful	Completely Successful
A solid rationale for change was provided			
Costs were predicted and an adequate ROI was determined			
The leaders of the change were willing volunteers			
A shared vision was created			
Commitment to change was created			
Everyone who wanted to be involved had an opportunity			
The right people were selected for the teams			
A comprehensive implementation plan for the change was prepared			
The change focused on results not activities			
Changes were completed with a minimum of interruption to the workforce			
Customers experienced no interruption of services			
Employees received training, development, and coaching as needed			
The change can be linked directly with the organizational strategic plan			
Monitoring and adjusting occurred in response to problems in the process			
Progress was tracked and published			
Clear success metrics were identified			
Change has been institutionalized with formal policies, systems, and structures			
Top management is committed to continued success of the change			
Employees are pleased with the results			

Activity 22. Helping Employees Succeed with Change (Appendix B)

Purpose: Provide "Success Guides" to employees.

Process:

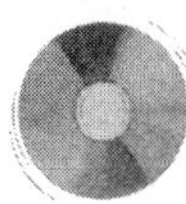

1. Make copies of the "Employees' Success Guide to Change" for everyone; this guide is found as appendix B of this book and on the accompanying CD as an editable Microsoft Word document. There is a great deal of flexibility with how to use the guide.
2. You may wish to deliver them one-to-one, through their supervisors, or in a workshop format.
3. The guides are self-paced, but you may wish to work through some of the activities as a group.
4. Whatever you choose, be sure that employees know that the guide is intended to help them succeed both during and after the change process.

Worksheet 11-16. Lessons Learned for Leaders

Review each of these statements and rate them in the first column using the following scale (and numbers in between): 0 = not at all—must have forgotten; 3 = pretty darn average and I need improvement; 6 = completely—didn't miss a beat.

Add your comments in the third column.

To what extent did you:

0–6	Skills and Behaviors	Comments
	Provide information early and often to employees?	
	Model behavior expected of others?	
	Clearly explain the reason for the change?	
	Focus on results?	
	Help employees understand what's in it for them?	
	Build a team trusted by the organization?	
	Set expectations for continuous change?	
	Create stories and paint a future vision?	
	Engineer some quick wins?	
	Encourage others to participate?	
	Listen to individuals for facts and feelings?	
	Provide all resources required?	
	Give others credit?	
	Provide recognition for small and large wins?	
	Continue to be upbeat and positive?	
	Help to address resistance?	
	Empathize with others' needs and concerns?	
	Manage the transition effectively?	
	Identify ways to symbolize the new identity?	
	Address the change from a systems approach?	
	Find ways to celebrate?	
	Participate in the evaluation?	

What strengths do you think you displayed during the change effort?

Activity 23. Lessons Learned for Leaders (Chapter 9)

Purpose: Provide an opportunity for leaders to evaluate their change management skills.

Process:

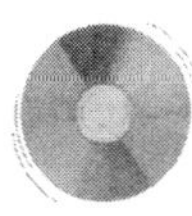

1. Share the self-evaluation in worksheet 11-16 with your leader (also available on the CD accompanying this volume). Suggest that the two of you complete the form and then discuss it.
2. Be sure to be honest and candid. It is the only way the leader can learn.
3. Consider planning a follow-up meeting for continuous learning.

Appendix A

Organizational Change Glossary

Note: Cross-referenced terms are in italics. Several of these definitions are found in ASTD's *AOE 5 Study Guide* or are based on the ASTD Learning System.

Action Research and Learning. This is both a model and a *process*. In its simplest form, it is a process whereby research or fact finding precedes action and follows it. The thought process looks something like this: fact finding—action—fact finding—action, and so on. The action research process takes shape as understanding increases. The process remains focused on the desired state and how each systemic element needs to change.

advocacy. Persuading others to follow or support a new *strategy*, *vision*, and/or initiative. This is the highest level of *commitment* to change—above awareness, acceptance, and adoption.

Appreciative Inquiry. A theory of large-scale organizational change that involves the analysis of positive and successful (rather than negative or failing) operations. The four-D cycle (discovery, dream, design, destiny) includes identifying problems, analyzing causes, searching for solutions, and developing an action plan.

buy-in. A measure of support for a new *vision*, *strategy*, and/or initiative that is synonymous with *commitment*; it has four levels: awareness, acceptance, adoption, and *advocacy*.

champions. People or groups that lead change.

change management. A school of thought pertaining to the creation and implementation of a new *vision*, *strategy*, and/or initiative whose principles help businesses take steps to maximize *commitment* and minimize resistance to change.

Chaos and Complexity Theory. A scientific theory that is applied to organizational development in an attempt to find order in the organizational environment.

Chaos Theory. The study of how a simple *system* can generate complicated behavior.

closed-ended, or direct, questions. These questions help to check for understanding or to test for consensus. They are sometimes preferable to open-ended questions to limit information.

commitment. A measure of support for a new *vision*, *strategy*, and/or initiative.

communication plans. Require identifying information and communication needs of stakeholders, the message, the method of delivery, and the timeline.

competency. A skill and level of expertise pertaining to a job.

complex system. A type of *system* that has details whose role in the larger system cannot be fully understood unless they are examined together with the system. By carefully studying the whole system, patterns can be identified.

complexity. The study of how a complicated *system* generates simple behavior.

confirmative evaluation. Provides the intermediate and long-term information to demonstrate that the desired future state is occurring. Continuing results are measured against expected results.

disaster scenario. A technique used to generate a strong sense of urgency by communicating the dire consequences of business as usual.

emotional intelligence. This is an "eighth intelligence" based on Gardner's Multiple Intelligence Theory, which suggests an ability to accurately identify and understand one's own emotional reactions and those of others, and is related to personal qualities, such as self-confidence and motivation. The theory was developed by Daniel Goleman in the 1990s and popularized in his book *Working with Emotional Intelligence.*

espoused values. The public expression of organizational *values*.

expectancy theory. Holds that people are motivated to work toward rewards that they want and that they believe they have a reasonable chance of obtaining.

experiential learning. Occurs when a learner participates in an activity, reviews the activity, identifies useful knowledge or skills that were gained, and transfers the result to the workplace.

experiential learning activities. Part of the *experiential learning* cycle that explains what must occur during an activity to ensure maximum learning occurs. The five steps are experiencing, publishing, processing, generalizing, and applying.

external environment. The constantly changing collection of forces outside the organization that influences business performance. These forces constrain the organization and define key business opportunities.

Five-Why Technique. A *process* to identify the root cause of a problem by asking consecutive "why" questions to avoid treating a symptom.

flat management model. A model in which the line of authority flows from the top to the lower levels of the organization. On each level, managers have authority over their areas (for example, credit and human resources managers) and their subordinates, who in turn have authority over others, and so on. Every employee reports to a single immediate superior.

flavor-of-the-month syndrome. The tendency of individuals in organizations to discount the significance of a new *vision*, *strategy*, and/or initiative; a barrier to the acceptance of change efforts.

focus group. A method for gathering qualitative information from a small group of people.

force field analysis. A diagnostic tool developed by Kurt Lewin to identify favorable and unfavorable effects when implementing change.

formal organization. An organizational *system,* structure, and/or *process* that supports day-to-day operations and allows organizations to produce an output.

4-D model. The approach used in appreciative inquiry consisting of four phases: discovery, dream, design, destiny.

goal-setting theory. Holds that people are best motivated when they participate in setting their own goals.

hierarchical management model. Divides larger tasks into smaller ones that people with little or no education could carry out. As first implemented by Henry Ford, decision making was shifted to a group of forepersons, supervisors, and managers.

high-performance organizations. Entities that establish and sustain vast economic, operational, and market performance.

incremental change. Change occurring on a regular basis as organizations attempt to keep pace with the evolving *external environment.* Also known as continuous change.

intervention. Another name for a solution or set of solutions—usually a combination of tools and techniques—that are directly related to solving a performance gap.

leadership development. Focuses on learning events—such as mentoring, training, self-study, and job rotation—that prepare employees to lead an organization.

Maslow's hierarchy of needs. Introduced in 1954 by Abraham Maslow in his book *Motivation and Personality.* He contended that people have complex needs that they strive to fulfill and that change and evolve over time. He categorized these needs as physiological (food, drink, sex, and sleep), safety/security, social/belongingness, esteem, and self-actualization, with the basic needs having to be satisfied before an individual can focus on growth.

matrix model. A model of management that combines line and project structures with a general manager at the top of the hierarchy. The purpose of matrix structures is to integrate diverse areas of expertise.

milestones. Key dates in a project when an event will occur. By setting milestones, change facilitators can track when key actions should occur.

motivation theory. Based on the idea that by creating the right work environment for people, they will be motivated to grow and become connected to that environment.

open-ended questions. Questions to stimulate discussion that have no one specific "correct" answer and encourage individuals to draw on their own experiences and apply them to the current situation or discussion.

open systems theory. Based on the idea that things in a *system* influence each other, or that groups of people (in an organization) learn from one another. Also known as "living" or "general" systems theory.

organizational culture. The unspoken pattern of those *values,* attitudes, and beliefs that guide the behavior of the people in an organization, including those that can be difficult to change.

organizational development (OD). The *process* of developing an organization to be more effective in achieving it business goals. OD utilizes planned interventions to develop the *system*, structure, and/or *process* within the organization to improve effectiveness.

position power. Power derived from formal reporting relationships and the ability to secure resources.

process. A set of sequenced activities that produce an output. Defines how products become produced, how services get delivered, and how information is distributed and used.

reengineering. A change movement popular in the early 1990s that promised increased efficiency and profitability through the implementation of advanced information management techniques and the redesign of a work *process*.

resisters. Individuals or groups that resist and disrupt change.

return-on-investment (ROI). A ratio of the benefit or profit received from a given investment to the cost of the investment itself. It constitutes accountability for training programs.

risk management plan. A *process* within project management that identifies, analyzes, and plans for potential risk.

scope creep. The tendency for a project to expand beyond its parameters affecting the timeline, budget, and resources available.

sender-receiver model. Postulates that communication between two people goes through each person's filters.

Seven-S Framework. Portrays the seven connected core elements of an organization—including structure, *system*, style, staff, skills, and *strategy*—displayed in a circle around the center, shared *values*. Identified with McKinsey.

Six Sigma methodology. A *process*-improvement *strategy* and measure of quality that strives for near perfection. Six Sigma is a disciplined, data-driven methodology for eliminating defects (driving toward six standard deviations between the mean and the nearest specification limit) in a *process*. The fundamental objective of the Six Sigma methodology is the implementation of a measurement-based *strategy* that focuses on process improvement and variation reduction through the application to projects.

stakeholder. An individual or group holding an interest in an issue.

strategy. A framework—more detailed than a *vision*—that guides day-to-day operational decision making on issues such as market definition; product/service definition; *commitment* to a certain *system*, structure, and/or *process*; and competitive differentiation.

success syndrome. The tendency of organizations and individuals to be lulled into complacency by a history of success.

SWOT (strengths, weaknesses, opportunities, threats) analysis. An assessment of a firm's internal environment and *external environment* that identifies internal strengths and weaknesses as well as opportunities and threats posed by external forces.

symptom. Something that signals the existence of a problem but not the problem's root cause.

system. An organizational *process* that supports day-to-day operations for compensation, information, and the like.

systems thinking. A conceptual framework that encompasses a whole *system*, making patterns (and ways to change them) more understandable.

Theory X. The traditional way of looking at the workforce, which assumes that people would rather play than work.

Theory Y. Postulates that most people will work to achieve goals to which they are committed, especially if rewards result from the achievement of those objectives, and that most people can learn to accept—and even seek—responsibility.

timelines. Graphic representations of the estimated duration of tasks and the project or of the *change management* effort as a whole.

town hall. A meeting open to all the employees of an organization, usually to discuss issues of general concern.

values. An element of an organization consisting of a set of beliefs defining right and wrong.

vision. A description of a desired end state; a foundation for a new *strategy* and/or initiative.

Weisbord's Six-Box Model. A framework developed by Marvin Weisbord that examines how organizations and rapidly changing sociotechnical environments influence each other simultaneously. It views tasks and *process* through six lenses: purpose, structure, relationships, rewards, helpful mechanisms, and leadership within the context of outside forces (environmental demands).

Appendix B

Employees' Success Guide to Change

Note to the Reader: This chapter is intended to be a guide for employees to explore their thoughts and feelings as they experience the change process. It is not filled with content but rather with questions and ideas to guide an employee through the chaos of change. It also provides a legitimate path to the top for employees who want to be a part of the change effort.

Please feel free to make copies of it and share it with your employees. Before you do, you may wish to tailor it to your company. The Microsoft Word version of this appendix on the CD that accompanies this book will allow you to add or change information in the guide; for instance:

- ✓ You can substitute your organization's name wherever the text says "organization."
- ✓ Space is available on the first page to describe the change your organization is encountering.
- ✓ You can add resources to the last page that will help employees. For example, there is space for you to list a hotline phone number for information, a website referencing the change, and a contact person in HR.
- ✓ Feel free to remove topics that do not resonate with your organization.
- ✓ Likewise, you can add tools that your organization has already introduced to the workforce.
- ✓ Finally, you can add appropriate names, phone numbers, and email addresses—for example, where the guide suggests contacting the "implementation team."

Employees' Success Guide to Change

Change is exhilarating when done by us,
and exasperating when done to us.
—Rosabeth Moss Kanter

"The only constant is change." An overused oxymoron? Maybe, but we know it is true. Change is always around us and is often difficult to accept and adapt to. In a short time, our organization will embark on a change journey. We are convinced the change is necessary and good for us.

We are completing a business case for the change that we will share with you shortly. In the meantime, we want to provide you with this copy of the "Employees' Success Guide to Change." Though people might perhaps more commonly speak of a *survival* guide than a success guide, as you can see, we've made the title say *success* because we want you to do more than merely survive the change. We want you to thrive. We want you to succeed!

This "Employees' Success Guide to Change" can help you succeed in several ways:

- ✓ Explain the change process to you.
- ✓ Assist you to explore your own ideas about change.
- ✓ Present activities to help you think about change.
- ✓ Give you tools and techniques to deal with the change.

This guide has been provided as a resource, and you are free to use it in any way that works best for you:

- ✓ You can start at page 1 and work through the guide to the end.
- ✓ You can open to any page, read the content, and complete the activities.
- ✓ You can use the guide as a resource whenever a need arises.

In any case, we hope you'll find it helpful as you travel the change journey with us.

Please don't hesitate to contact your supervisor or anyone on your change implementation team if you have questions.

Happy reading,

Change Implementation Team

You and Change

Everyone responds differently to change. Some get excited about it. Some dread it. Some just go along with it because there's nothing much you can do about it.

Your attitude about change is important. How you react to change determines the impact change will have on you. No one controls how you respond to change—just you.

Think about the last change you went through. It could have been a personal or professional change.

What did you think, and how did you feel about the change?

____

____

What happened that made the change difficult or easy?

____

____

What do you wish would have happened?

____

____

How did you deal with the change? Is this the way you usually deal with change? Or was there something different about this instance?

____

____

List three words that describe how you address change.

____

____

____

You will find a list of quotes on the next page. Circle a couple that resonate with you. What do you think this tells you about how you approach change?

____

____

Quote Me

- "Change is constant." —Benjamin Disraeli
- "If you want to truly understand something, try to change it." —Kurt Lewin
- "When the drumbeat changes, the dance changes." —Hausa People
- "Opportunities are never lost. The other fellow takes those you miss." —Anonymous
- "If the window of opportunity appears, don't pull the shade down." —Tom Peters
- "High expectations are the key to everything." —Sam Walton
- "Determine that the thing can and shall be done, and we shall find the way." —Abraham Lincoln
- "Change your thoughts and you change your world." —Norman Vincent Peale
- "The way I see it, if you want the rainbow, you must put up with the rain." —Dolly Parton
- "I never think of the future; it comes soon enough." —Albert Einstein
- "If there were none who were discontented with what they have, the world would never reach for anything better." —Florence Nightingale
- "One change makes way for the next, giving us the opportunity to grow." —Vivian Buchan
- "Dig a well before you are thirsty." —Chinese proverb
- "All birth is unwilling." —Pearl S. Buck
- "Neither situations nor people can be altered by the interference of an outsider; it must come from within." —Phyllis Bottome
- "You must do the thing you think you cannot do." —Eleanor Roosevelt
- "Life is either a daring adventure or nothing." —Helen Keller
- "Before you change your thinking, you have to change what goes into your mind." —Anonymous
- "A habit cannot be tossed out the window; it must be coaxed down the stairs a step at a time." —Mark Twain
- "Our stomachs quiver at the prospects of change. But today's leaders and managers have no choice." —Robert Waterman
- "Progress is not created by contented people." —F. Tyger
- "Why not go out on a limb? That's where the fruit is." —Will Rogers
- "It is one thing to learn from the past; it is another to wallow in it." —Kenneth Auchincloss
- "It is not the strongest of the species that survive, nor the most intelligent, but the one most responsive to change." —Charles Darwin
- "We must become the change we want to see." —Mahatma Gandhi
- "We don't see things as they are. We see things as we are." —Anaïs Nin

What Do You Want?

When an organization implements a change effort, employees have expectations for what they would like to see happen. What would you like to occur? Use the grid below to capture what you would like us to do. Simply mark an X in the column for "yes," "no," or "not sure."

What do I want?	Yes	No	Not Sure
I want to know the organization's vision for the future.			
I want lots of communication.			
I want to know the reason for the change.			
I want to know how this will affect my job.			
I want to know what is going to be better.			
I want to know what is going to be worse.			
I would like to hear the bad news as well as the good news.			
I want to participate in the planning.			
I want to participate in the implementation.			
I want to be able to give feedback to management.			
I want to know who can answer my questions.			
I want to know more about the transition plan.			
I want to know the timeline.			
I would like to know what part I will play in the change.			
I would like to know how we will measure our success.			

We are operating under the assumption that you will mark more yes's than no's. If we are incorrect, please let us know.

What else would you like to know?

Please communicate this to your supervisor or the implementation team. We are committed to keeping you informed. Let us know if we have not met your needs and how we can do better.

The CHANGE Model

Change is a very messy process. To help keep us organized, we are using a six-step CHANGE Model. The process creates a road map for us to follow from initiation through evaluation. We are aware, however, that change is rarely the nice, neat, linear process that is presented in this model. Sometimes the steps overlap, and sometimes we may be working on two different steps at the same time. That is in part due to the very nature of change—and because we won't always have all the answers.

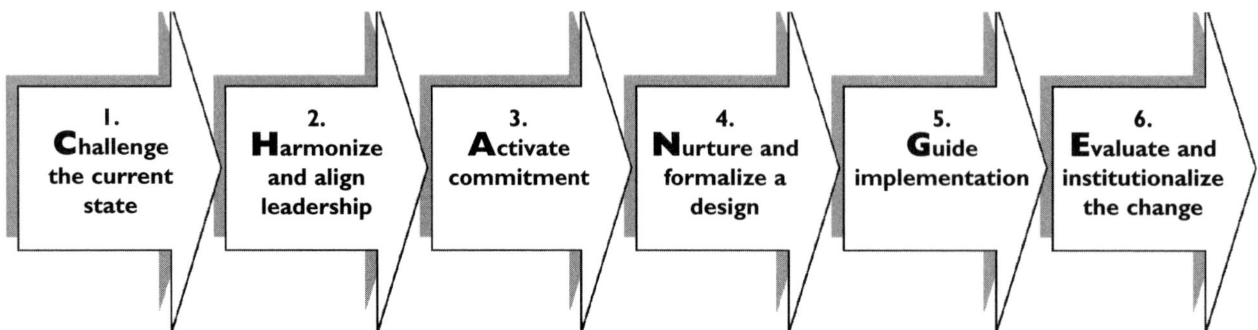

Every organization is different, and so every change intervention will be different. Each of the steps does, however, provide you with a general idea of what will be happening.

Step 1: Challenge the current state. This step addresses the recognition that something can be better, a preferred future that dares the status quo to innovate. This step is usually initiated by someone at or near the top of the organization who identifies a need for change. It may be externally generated, such as an impending industry regulation. Or it may be internally generated, such as a high percentage of retirement-eligible personnel on the horizon. This step addresses the question of "why?" Why do we need to do this?

Step 2: Harmonize and align leadership. This step focuses on aligning the organization's leadership to understand the organizational need and to identify a way to focus on the challenge from a systems perspective. It is also leadership's responsibility to create the vision for the future and model the expectation. You can expect leaders to begin to communicate with the rest of the organization about what will happen and why. This step addresses the question of "what?" What do we need to do?

Step 3: Activate commitment. At this step, teams are formed to begin to design, the implementation. Employees are involved to consider what to keep, what to change, and how to change. Leaders continue to communicate to ensure that everyone knows what is happening and understands how the change will occur. This step answers the question of "how?" How will we conduct the change effort?

Step 4: Nurture and formalize a design. This step ensures that the plans in the last step are the correct ones, that resources are available, and that everyone is on board to begin transitioning to the preferred future state. Many organizations skip the first three steps and begin their change effort at this point. They decide a change must take place and then begin to create the change. Unfortunately, this approach rarely works. As part of this step, we will conduct a risk assessment, select appropriate metrics, and utilize a number of implementation tools.

Step 5: Guide implementation. This step is where all the action occurs. Many people throughout our organization will be busy creating new processes and coordinating with people in other departments to keep the implementation moving forward. We will be looking for proof that we are doing the right thing for you and all our employees. We will call them short-term wins. We hope everyone, including you, will be on board with the change.

Step 6: Evaluate and institutionalize the change. Once the implementation has been completed, many organizations are off to find other dragons to slay. Instead, we will evaluate what we did to identify lessons learned for the future. We will also be focused on ensuring that the change is permanently institutionalized, and we hope you will help us with this step.

We are excited about the process we will use, and we invite you to join us in this important and exciting journey for our organization.

How would you like to be involved? Please let one of the members of the change management team know.

To learn more about implementing a change initiative, read John Kotter's book *Leading Change.* (Full information on this and all other materials for further reading is given at the end of the guide.)

Changes and Decisions

"Who are you?" said the Caterpillar. . . .
"I—I hardly know, Sir, just at present," Alice replied rather shyly,
"at least I know who I was when I got up this morning, but I think
I must have been changed several times since then."
—Lewis Carroll

Like Alice in Lewis Carroll's *Alice's Adventures in Wonderland*, you may feel as if you have been changed several times in a day at work. Decisions made by you or someone else make your well-planned day go awry. Decisions and change go hand in hand.

Decisions in a change effort often require people to leave something behind or to bypass tempting alternatives. By recognizing the continual need to make choices during our organizational change, we can all see that a big change for the organization is really a series of smaller manageable choices. That is perhaps why it sometimes feels as if there are lots of changes occurring every day.

When was the last time you read Robert Frost's poem "The Road Not Taken" (you can find it on the Internet at www.bartleby.com/119/1). Read it and think about some of the passages and phrases, such as "looked down one as far as I could" and "doubted if I should ever come back." How does this poem reflect your life? Work? The change effort we are currently implementing? What lessons are here for you as we continue down the road on our change journey?

Throughout your life, you have made many decisions, gone down many roads, taken a few detours, and maybe even fallen down a rabbit hole! In most cases, you were probably most satisfied when you made the decisions yourself.

We believe you will be more satisfied with our change effort if you are involved and a part of the decision making. We want you to be A-W-A-R-E of the process:

Aware of what we are planning

Willing to participate in this new direction

Able and knowledgeable about how to support the change

Ready to implement the change when the time is right

Enthusiastically encouraging others to be a part of the vision.

AWARE: Not Just Another Acronym

AWARE is not just another acronym. We have tried to think of what you require to be successful with the current change effort. Let's take a look at the organization's commitment to you.

Aware of what we are planning: We are committed to providing you with plenty of communication. We want you to be in the know. We are preparing a communication plan that will deliver information through numerous channels. We are counting on you to tell us how well the communication is working.

What can you do to help?

____

____

Willing to participate in this exciting direction: We know we can't just communicate. We need to ensure that you truly understand what we are doing; that you have a clear picture of the vision; that you know why this is important to the company, to you, and to the rest of the workforce; and that you know how we intend to create this change.

What can you do to help?

____

____

Able and knowledgeable about how to support the change: We are committed to providing you with the skills and knowledge for your role in the organization. Tell us what skills and knowledge you need to support the change. Identify the skill gaps so that we can provide training, coaching, job aids, and whatever else you need as soon as possible.

What can you do to help?

____

____

Ready to implement when the time is right: We hope that you will be as conscious and knowledgeable of the timeline as we are. Help us keep the momentum up from an organizational perspective as well as from your personal perspective. We want you to be prepared to slip into your new role when the time is right. What challenges do you see?

What can you do to help?

____

____

Enthusiastically encouraging others to be a part of the vision: Finally, we hope that you will go beyond your corner of the world and help us help others to get on board. What motivates you? What motivates others? Tell us how we can help you with this task.

What can you do to help?

____

____

We want you to be AWARE that we are here to help you with the change.

We Have a Vision—but I Can't See It!

A vision statement should serve as the guiding light to employees, describing the preferred future that the change will create. It is more than words on a laminated card. A vision statement paints a picture of where an organization wants to be in 3, 5, 10, 50 years. It creates urgency and draws people in. And it inspires.

Employees need to see and understand the future. They need a target at which to aim. People are more supportive and willing to help create something that they understand. However, sometimes organizations write vision statements that are not easily understood by everyone.

Our leaders need to create scenarios for employees, painting a picture that everyone can understand. They need to map out a strategy that gives the vision life. Think about our vision statement.

1. What is our vision for the future?

2. What does our vision statement mean?

3. Can you see, hear, feel, touch, and taste the new organization in our vision?

4. Can you clearly describe why we need to move in the direction of the vision?

If you cannot positively answer the four questions above, please talk with your supervisor or contact a member of the implementation team.

What Can You Do If You're Not Sure?

You are now almost halfway through this guide. What if you're just not sure about your involvement or commitment? It probably means we have not done the job we need to do.

Do you need answers to these questions or others?

- Tell me again, why are we doing this?
- What's in it for me (WIIFM)?
- How do I fit into the vision?
- What choices do I have?
- Will I have a job?
- What if I cannot perform the new job?
- What if I do not want to change?
- If I wait long enough, will this change go away?
- What do you expect me to do to support the change?
- Who can answer my questions?
- ?
- ?
- ?
- ?

If you have these questions, others undoubtedly do too. Obviously, we have not adequately answered them for you. Uncertainty can cloud the workplace and prevent you from doing the kind of job you'd like to do. Make a list of all your concerns and questions. Then turn to the next page to identify how you would like to get your questions answered.

Address Your Uncertainty

Not sure how to address your uncertainty? With your list of questions in hand, here are our best suggestions for getting the information you need:

- Identify someone who seems to be positive and in the know. Invite the individual to go to lunch and take your list with you.
- Perhaps you already have the information and you have simply encountered doubts through other people or through your own thought process. If so, use a "what's good about it" scenario. Ask yourself to imagine that the change goes as planned. Ask what's good about it.
- Take your list of questions to your supervisor and ask for the information you need. Don't be surprised if your supervisor does not have all the answers. If you don't know, others may not either.
- Check to learn if the implementation team has a "hotline," question box, or some other communication process for answering these questions.
- Find out the names of the implementation team's members. Make an appointment to talk with one of them.
- Check the communication plan to learn when the next general information session is scheduled. Attend with your questions in hand. Select your two most burning issues to ask about.

What else can you do to get your questions answered?

What Can We Do Better?

Organizations can prevent change from feeling uncomfortable and threatening.

William Bridges, the change expert and author of *Managing Transitions*, says that if employees are to feel comfortable with change, they need these four Ps:

- Purpose, or the reasons for the change.
- Picture of the expected outcome.
- Plan for navigating from the current situation to the future.
- Part the employee will play in making the changes successful.

Think about the current change effort our organization is implementing. How would you grade us on Bridges's four Ps? For each, would we get an A, B, C, D, or F?

_____ Purpose, or the reasons for the change.

_____ Picture of the expected outcome.

_____ Plan for navigating from the current situation to the future.

_____ Part the employee will play in making the changes successful.

Why did you give the grades you did?

____

____

What recommendations do you have for management to make the change more acceptable to employees?

____

____

What could you do differently to help ensure success?

____

____

How can you share your thoughts with management?

____

____

Ideas to Keep You Involved and Learning

Do you want to be more involved in the change effort? Try one or more of these:

- Volunteer to help the implementation team.
- If your boss is helping with the implementation, ask how you can assist with some of the other projects on his or her desk.
- Attend informational meetings, town hall meetings, and other events, and listen for ways in which you could get involved.
- Volunteer to write some of the communication pieces that are delivered to the workforce, for example, newsletter articles, emails, flyers, posters, and other materials the committee produces.
- Join with others who want to learn more about the change process and read either *Who Moved My Cheese?* or *Our Iceberg Is Melting*. Meet to discuss the book and compare it with our organization.
- Visit the Our Iceberg Is Melting website (www.ouricebergismelting.com) for questions to stimulate discussion in the group mentioned in the previous suggestion or to stimulate your own thinking.
- Invite someone to attend your staff meeting (of course, if it is your boss's staff meeting, check it out first) to provide an update about the change effort. Have a stack of index cards available for questions from the group.
- Provide open and honest feedback to the implementation team—good, bad, or neutral—we need to know.
- Read some of the books in the resource section of this guide.
- Identify a stretch task in your department and ask your supervisor to assign it to you.
- Ask yourself, "What skills and knowledge would I like to have next year at this time?"
- List other things you could do:

____

____

Summarize What You've Learned

The reason we need to change is

____

____

The opportunities that exist include

____

____

The benefits to me include

____

____

The skills to successfully travel the change journey include

____

____

What strengths do you bring to our organization's change effort?

____

____

What strengths do you need to acquire?

____

____

Your plan to gain skills and knowledge for your new role includes

____

____

Oh, the Places You'll Go!

I'm sorry to say so
but, sadly, it's true
that Bang-ups
and Hang-ups
can happen to you.
—Dr. Seuss, *Oh, the Places You'll Go!*

When was the last time you read a Dr. Seuss book? Well, that's your task. Find a copy of his book *Oh, the Places You'll Go!*, read it (it's more fun with a little friend!), and answer the questions in the next paragraphs.

In the book, characters react and respond to change differently:

- The path to change is either difficult or fun.
- The road to change may be a scary experience or a confusing one.
- The experience can be one that you hope will go away or one that evokes responsibility to get it done.
- Change can be an exciting open road or a speed bump to avoid.

1. Depending upon how long you have had this guide, and how involved you are in the change process, how would you gauge your feelings about the change in our organization on a 7-point scale. Place an X where you think you are:

Pleased						**Disappointed**
1	2	3	4	5	6	7

2. What caused you to place your X where you did?

____

____

3. If your X was on the 1, great! Tell us what we need to do to keep you there.

____

____

4. If your X was anywhere except the 1, tell us what we need to do to move it to the left.

____

____

5. Have you thought about the skills you need to be better involved in pursuing the new vision? Please let us know what skills and knowledge you need. We'd love to hear about them.

Holding On and Letting Go

Sometimes things happen during the change process that continue to nag at us. We just can't seem to let them go. This exercise will help you figure out why an issue is bothering you and what you want to do about it. Find a quiet spot where you will not be disturbed for 30 minutes or so. Identify a concern that you just can't seem to let go—that is, not let it bother you anymore. Using the matrix below, identify all the advantages and disadvantages for holding on to it and all the advantages and disadvantages for letting it go. Then answer the questions on the next page.

Issue: ____

	Holding On	Letting Go
Advantages		
Disadvantages		

Holding On and Letting Go (Continued)

1. What did you discover as you completed the Holding On and Letting Go matrix?

2. In what ways could you minimize the positive reasons for holding on?

3. In what ways could you strengthen the advantages of letting go?

4. What made this exercise difficult?

5. What did you learn from this exercise?

6. What will you do differently as a result of this exercise?

You may not have reached any final decisions about your issue, but we hope this exercise helped you put what is keeping you from moving on in perspective. You may wish to speak with someone whose opinion you value to help you continue to address this issue.

Did You Hear the Latest Rumor?

"Did you hear we're going to do all of their work too!"

"Did you hear that they're planning to cut our pay?"

"Did you hear that the VP of finance is so fed up that he's leaving?"

"Did you hear . . ."

Rumors abound during any change initiative. Why do they get started? There are many reasons, including

- limited information from management, which is misinterpreted.
- fear about the unknown, so people play a "what if" game.
- a lack of communication, so employees "fill in the blanks."
- anger that routines may be changed, which makes people strike out verbally.
- anxiety about uncertainties, which creates a void that needs to be filled.

Keep in mind that rumors may prevent people from moving forward. Perhaps you could help implement one of these ways to address rumors that may be buzzing around you:

- Use a Dear Abby approach called "Rose Rogers," who wears, of course, rose-colored glasses.
- Post FAQs on the organization's website.
- Use a toll-free "fact or fiction" phone number to ask for and to get answers.
- Have a Rumor of the Week contest.
- Deal with rumors up front by saying "This is what you don't need to worry about."

How do rumors affect your attitude?

What action do you need to take to maintain a positive attitude?

How do you perceive the change at this time?

Negativity

In addition to rumors, you may encounter negative attitudes. For negative people, the glass isn't half full. It isn't even half empty. It is broken!

Negativity is contagious. Be cautious that you do not catch the negativity bug. What can you do about negativity?

- Keep your distance from negative people.
- Change the subject to something more positive.
- Suggest the positive side of the issue.
- If the negativity centers on "can't," ask "Why not?"
- Don't ignore negativity completely; perhaps the person has a valid point that needs to be addressed. Take the concern to someone in the know.

How can you help someone overcome a negative attitude? Try these ideas:

- Discuss the benefits of supporting the change. You might include increased professional growth, enhanced job security, and satisfaction in knowing you are helping the organization. What others can you think of?
  - —
  - —
  - —
  - —
- Release any energy that might be creating the negativity by asking the people expressing the concern to complete sentences such as "I am afraid the change effort will . . ." and "This change will only be successful if . . ."
- In conversation, try a creative approach, such as asking the person to view the change from the customer's perspective or to view the change 10 years from now. What does he or she see looking at it from another perspective?
- Finally, here's a helpful process you can use in many situations to SHIFT someone's negativity, resistance, or pessimism. Just follow these steps that spell S-H-I-F-T:

  Surface the resistance by making it safe to express it; listen carefully and be certain that you understand the root cause.

  Honor the resistance by affirming the person's right to resist; reassure that you understand, letting the person know that you appreciate the insight.

  Identify the kind of resistance; differentiate between current resistance and former grudges, and between resentment and a need for attention.

  Find out what the resister would prefer and begin to work toward a common objective. Check the status to learn if any agreement has been reached.

  Thank the person and move on. You will not be able to turn everyone around, though this SHIFT process often works.

Pack a New Bag for Our Change Journey

What will you include in your new change bag?

What skills are necessary to be an employee who embraces change?

What have you learned? What do you still need to learn?

Change Review Crossword Puzzle

ACROSS

1 What our organization will go through
3 Most important during change
8 Opposite of positive
10 A vision should do this
12 False information
13 Author of book, *Leading Change*
14 Number of steps in the change process

DOWN

1 First word of the first step
2 Our company wants you to do this
4 Process to shift negativity
5 Change process is not neat
6 What's in it for me
7 Plan for the future
9 Acronym for employee success
11 One of the Bridges's 4 Ps

Crossword Puzzle Answers

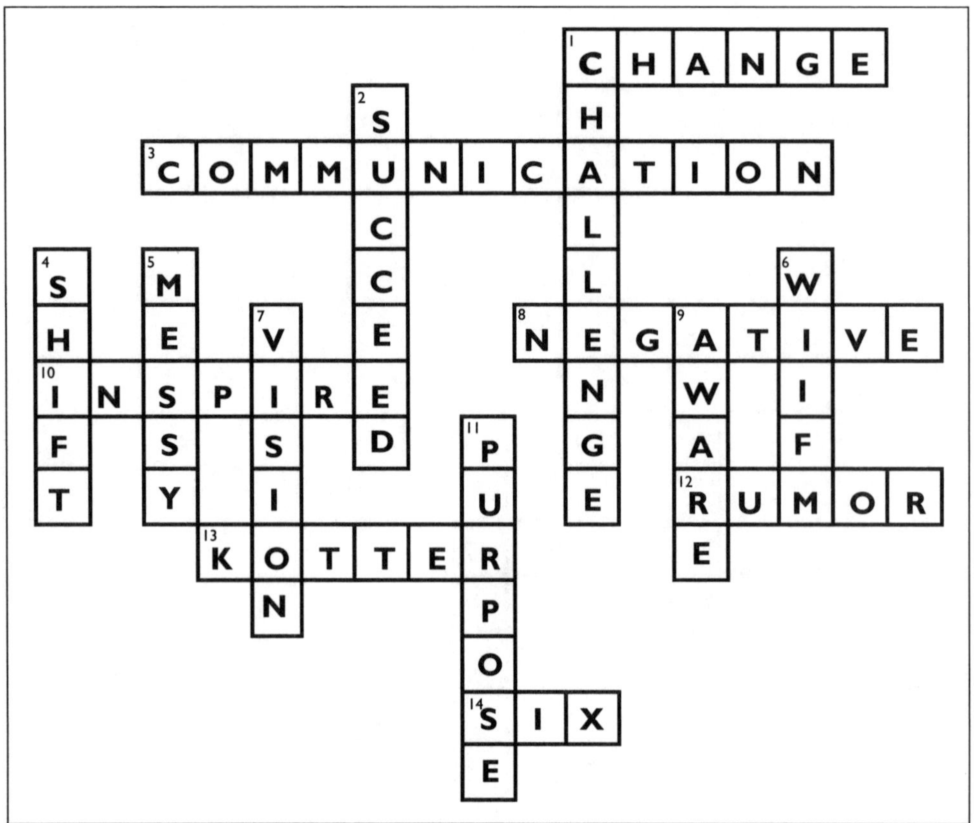

Reading and Resource List

There are many resources to help you with the change. The ones mentioned above and several others we rely on are listed here. If you find others, be sure to share them with your colleagues.

Books

Block, Peter. *The Empowered Manager: Positive Political Skills at Work.* San Francisco: Jossey-Bass/Pfeiffer, 1987.

Bridges, William. *Transitions: Making Sense of Life's Changes.* Reading, MA: Addison-Wesley Publishing, 2004.

Collins, James C. *Good to Great: Why Some Companies Make the Leap . . . and Others Don't.* New York: HarperCollins, 2001.

Evans, Jeff, and Chuck Schaefer. *Ten Tasks of Change: Demystifying Changing Organizations.* San Francisco: Jossey-Bass/Pfeiffer, 2001.

Goleman, Daniel. *Working with Emotional Intelligence.* New York: Bantam Doubleday Dell, 1998.

Johnson, Spencer. *Who Moved My Cheese?* New York: G. P. Putnam's Sons, 1998.

Kotter, John. *Leading Change.* Boston: Harvard Business School Press, 1996.

Kotter, John P., and Dan S. Cohen. *The Heart of Change: Real-Life Stories of How People Change Their Organizations.* Boston: Harvard Business School Press, 2002.

Kotter, John, and Holger Rathgeber. *Our Iceberg Is Melting.* New York: St. Martin's Press, 2005.

Kouzes, James M., and Barry Z. Posner. *Encouraging the Heart: A Leader's Guide to Rewarding and Recognizing Others,* 4th ed. New York: Simon & Schuster, 2007.

Nelson, Bob. *1001 Ways to Reward Employees,* 2nd ed. New York: Workman, 2005.

Quinn, Robert E. *Deep Change: Discovering the Leader Within.* San Francisco: Jossey-Bass, 1996.

Other Resources

Your Human Resources Department

Your supervisor

Appendix C

Further Reading

This appendix includes both books and related ASTD *Infolines*.

Books

Because all the answers cannot reside in one book—or even several—I have included many books here. Although there is a great deal of crossover, volumes are grouped on the basis of how well their content matches the topics of each chapter and/or the chapter where they are mentioned. Thus a book may be listed more than once, for the reader's ease of reference while focusing on a particular chapter.

Overall Help

Beckhard, Richard, and Wendy Pritchard. *Changing the Essence: The Art of Creating and Leading Fundamental Change in Organizations*. San Francisco: Jossey-Bass, 1992.

Block, Peter. *Flawless Consulting: A Guide to Getting Your Expertise Used*. 2nd ed. San Francisco: Jossey-Bass/Pfeiffer, 1981.

Cohen, Dan S. *The Heart of Change Field Guide*. Boston: Harvard Business School Press, 2005.

Conner, Daryl R. *Managing at the Speed of Change*. New York: Random House, 1993.

Evans, Jeff, and Chuck Schaefer. *Ten Tasks of Change: Demystifying Changing Organizations*. San Francisco: Jossey-Bass/Pfeiffer, 2001.

Kotter, John P. *Leading Change*. Boston: Harvard Business School Press, 1996.

Chapter 1. Changing Times

Beer, Michael, and Nitin Nohria, eds. *Breaking the Code of Change*. Boston: Harvard Business School Press, 2000.

Bellman, Geoffrey M. *The Beauty of the Beast*. San Francisco: Berrett-Koehler, 2000.

Collins, James C., and Jerry Porras. *Built to Last: Successful Habits of Visionary Companies*. New York: Perseus Books, 1997.

McLagan, Pat. *Change Is Everyone's Business*. San Francisco: Berrett-Koehler, 2003.

Chapter 2. Facilitating Change

Biech, Elaine. *The Pfeiffer Book of Successful Team-Building Tools.* 2nd ed. San Francisco: Jossey-Bass/Pfeiffer, 2007.

———. *Training for Dummies.* Hoboken, NJ: Wiley, 2005.

Bellman, Geoffrey M. *The Consultant's Calling.* San Francisco: Jossey-Bass, 2002.

Gilley, Ann. *The Manager as Change Leader.* Westport, CT: Praeger, 2005.

Gottlieb, Marvin R. *Managing Group Process.* Westport, CT: Greenwood, 2003.

McCain, Donald, and Deborah Tobey. *Facilitation Basics.* Alexandria, VA: ASTD Press, 2004.

Rees, Fran. *The Facilitator Excellence Handbook.* San Francisco: Jossey-Bass/Pfeiffer, 1998.

Chapter 3. Models of Change

Albrecht, Karl. *Organization Development: A Total Systems Approach to Positive Change.* Upper Saddle River, NJ: Prentice-Hall, 1983.

Beer, Michael, and Nitin Nohria, eds. *Breaking the Code of Change.* Boston: Harvard Business School Press, 2000.

Cohen, Dan S. *The Heart of Change Field Guide.* Boston: Harvard Business School Press, 2005.

Cooperrider, David. *Appreciative Inquiry Handbook.* Bedford Heights, OH: Lake Shore Publishers, 2003.

Evans, Jeff, and Chuck Schaefer. *Ten Tasks of Change: Demystifying Changing Organizations.* San Francisco: Jossey-Bass/Pfeiffer, 2001.

Kotter, John P. *Leading Change.* Boston: Harvard Business School Press, 1996.

Lewin, Kurt. "Frontiers in Group Dynamics." *Human Relations* 1 (1951).

Nadler, David A. *Champions of Change: How CEOs and Their Companies Are Mastering the Skills of Radical Change.* San Francisco: Jossey-Bass, 1998.

Senge, Peter. *The Fifth Discipline.* New York: Doubleday, 1990.

Ulrich, David. *Human Resource Champions.* Boston: Harvard Business School Press, 1998.

Wheatley, Margaret J. *Leadership and the New Science: Learning about Organizations from an Orderly Universe.* San Francisco: Berrett-Koehler, 1992.

Chapter 4. Challenge the Current State (Step 1)

Bridges, William. *Managing Transitions: Making the Most of Change.* 2nd ed. Cambridge, MA: Da Capo Press, 2003.

Cohen, Dan S. *The Heart of Change Field Guide.* Boston: Harvard Business School Press, 2005.

Kotter, John P. *Leading Change.* Boston: Harvard Business School Press, 1996.

Maruska, Don. *How Great Decisions Get Made.* New York: AMACOM, 2004

Russell, Jeffrey, and Linda Russell. *Leading Change Training.* Alexandria, VA: ASTD Press, 2003.

Chapter 5. Harmonize and Align Leadership (Step 2)

Abrahams, Jeffrey. *Mission Statement Book: 301 Corporate Mission Statements from America's Top Companies.* Berkeley, CA: Ten Speed Press, 1999.

Collins, James C. *Good to Great: Why Some Companies Make the Leap . . . and Others Don't.* New York: HarperCollins, 2001.

Evans, Jeff, and Chuck Schaefer. *Ten Tasks of Change: Demystifying Changing Organizations.* San Francisco: Jossey-Bass/Pfeiffer, 2001.

Goleman, Daniel. *Working with Emotional Intelligence.* New York: Bantam Doubleday Dell, 1998.

Goodstein, Leonard David, Timothy Nolan, and J. William Pfeiffer. *Applied Strategic Planning: How to Develop a Plan That Really Works.* New York: McGraw-Hill, 1993.

Kotter, John, and Holger Rathgeber. *Our Iceberg Is Melting.* New York: St. Martin's Press, 2005.

Nadler, David A. *Champions of Change: How CEOs and Their Companies Are Mastering the Skills of Radical Change.* San Francisco: Jossey-Bass, 1998.

Phillips, Jack J., and Elwood F. Holton III. *Leading Organizational Change.* Alexandria, VA: ASTD Press, 1997.

Quinn, Robert E. *Deep Change: Discovering the Leader Within.* San Francisco: Jossey-Bass, 1996.

Weisbord, Marvin R., and Sandra Janoff. *Future Search: An Action Guide to Finding Common Ground in Organizations and Communities.* New York: Berrett-Koehler, 1999.

Chapter 6. Activate Commitment (Step 3)

Block, Peter. *Flawless Consulting: A Guide to Getting Your Expertise Used.* 2nd ed. San Francisco: Jossey-Bass/Pfeiffer, 2000.

Bridges, William. *Managing Transitions: Making the Most of Change.* 2nd ed. Cambridge, MA: Da Capo Press, 2003.

Galford, Robert, and Anne Seibold Drapeau. *The Trusted Leader.* New York: Free Press, 2002.

Maurer, Rick. *Beyond the Wall of Resistance.* Austin: Bard Books, 1996.

Rogers, Everett M. *Diffusion of Innovations.* 4th ed. New York: Free Press, 1995.

Chapter 7. Nurture and Formalize a Design (Step 4)

Bridges, William. *Managing Transitions: Making the Most of Change.* 2nd ed. Cambridge, MA: Da Capo Press, 2003.

Cohen, Dan S. *The Heart of Change Field Guide.* Boston: Harvard Business School Press, 2005.

Conner, Daryl R. *Managing at the Speed of Change.* New York: Random House, 1993.

Senge, Peter, et al. *The Fifth Discipline Fieldbook: Strategies and Tools for Building a Learning Organization.* New York: Doubleday/Currency, 1994.

Chapter 8. Guide Implementation (Step 5)

Biech, Elaine. *TQM for Training.* New York: McGraw-Hill, 1994.

Blanchard, Ken, and Spencer Johnson. *The One-Minute Manager.* New York: HarperCollins, 1981.

Conner, Daryl R. *Leading at the Edge of Chaos.* New York: John Wiley and Sons, 1998.

Kaye, Beverly, and Sharon Jordan-Evans. *Love 'Em or Lose 'Em.* 3rd ed. San Francisco: Berrett-Koehler, 2005.

Nelson, Bob. *1001 Ways to Reward Employees.* 2nd ed. New York: Workman, 2005.

Sujansky, Joanne. *The Keys to Putting Change in Your Pocket.* Pittsburgh: KeyGroup, 2001.

Chapter 9. Evaluate and Institutionalize the Change (Step 6)

Bellman, Geoffrey M. *The Beauty of the Beast.* San Francisco: Berrett-Koehler, 2000.

Kotter, John P., and Dan S. Cohen. *The Heart of Change: Real-Life Stories of How People Change Their Organizations.* Boston: Harvard Business School Press, 2002.

Kouzes, James M., and Barry Z. Posner. *Encouraging the Heart: A Leader's Guide to Rewarding and Recognizing Others.* 4th ed. New York: Simon & Schuster, 2007.

Sujansky, Joanne. *The Keys to Putting Change in Your Pocket.* Pittsburgh: KeyGroup, 2001.

Whitney, Diana, David Cooperrider, and Amanda Trosten-Bloom. *The Power of Appreciative Inquiry: A Practical Guide to Positive Change.* New York: Berrett-Koehler, 2002.

Chapter 10. Toward a Perspective on Change: The Big Picture and the Future

Block, Peter. *The Empowered Manager: Positive Political Skills at Work.* San Francisco: Jossey-Bass/Pfeiffer, 1987.

Kanter, Rosabeth Moss, Barry A. Stein, and Todd D. Jick. *The Challenge of Organizational Change: How Companies Experience It and Leaders Guide It.* New York: Free Press, 1992.

Senge, Peter. *The Fifth Discipline: The Art and Practice of the Learning Organization.* New York: Doubleday, 1990.

Chapter 11. Activities to Support the CHANGE Journey

Evans, Jeff, and Chuck Schaefer. *Ten Tasks of Change: Demystifying Changing Organizations.* San Francisco: Jossey Bass/Pfeiffer, 2001.

Nilson, Carolyn. *Games That Drive Change.* New York: McGraw-Hill, 1995.

Schmidt, Suzanne, and Joanne Sujansky. *Training Games for Managing Change.* New York: McGraw-Hill, 1999.

Related ASTD *Infolines*

Cadzow, L., and P. Lake. "Drive Change With Case Studies." *Infoline* 250211.

Cheney, S. "Benchmarking." *Infoline* 259801.

Cowan, S. L. "Change Management." *Infoline* 259904.

Darraugh, B., ed. "How to Motivate Employees." *Infoline* 259108.

———. "Understanding Reengineering: Organizational Transformation." *Infoline* 259308.

Estep, T. "Meetings that Work!" *Infoline* 250505.

———. "Organization Development for Trainers." *Infoline* 250411.

Johnson, J. "Ethics for Trainers." *Infoline* 250406.

Kamine, M., C. deMello-e-Souza Wildermuth, and R. Collins. "Diversity Programs That Work." *Infoline* 250312.

Koehle, D. "The Role of the Performance Change Manager." *Infoline* 259715.

Lauby, S. "Motivating Employees." *Infoline* 250510.

Marquardt, M. "Action Learning." *Infoline* 259704.

Murrell, K. "Organizational Culture." *Infoline* 259304.

Pietrzak, T. "Successful Inside Consulting." *Infoline* 250311.

Smith, W. "Managing Change: Implementation Skills." *Infoline* 258910.

Solomon, C. "Culture Audits: Supporting Organizational Success." *Infoline* 250412.

Titcomb, T. J. "Chaos and Complexity Theory." *Infoline* 259807.

VanTiem, D., and J. Rosenzweig. "Appreciative Inquiry." *Infoline* 250601.

Zulauf, C. A. "Systems Thinking." *Infoline* 259703.

Appendix D

Worksheets

- Worksheet 2-1
- Worksheet 4-1
- Worksheet 4-2
- Worksheet 4-3
- Worksheet 5-1
- Worksheet 5-2
- Worksheet 9-1
- Worksheet 9-2
- Worksheet 9-3

Worksheet 2-1. Change Management Skills Assessment

Here's an opportunity to rate your competency in each of the six CHANGE Model steps.

Use this 1–5 rating scale: 1 = no experience or skill; 2 = minimal ability; 3 = average ability; 4 = above-average ability; 5 = outstanding ability.

Challenge the current state:

___ Use a process to gather and analyze data.

___ Build a business case.

___ Implement actions to establish a sense of urgency.

___ Differentiate change management roles.

___ Determine organizational readiness for change.

Harmonize and align leadership:

___ Build trust and confidence in diverse people at all levels of the organization.

___ Select and build a change implementation team.

___ Coach change leaders about the required leadership qualities.

___ Facilitate a process to create a compelling change vision.

___ Design a communication plan.

Activate commitment:

___ Attain buy-in to the vision.

___ Design an implementation based on solid theory.

___ Define and predict reactions to change.

___ Build critical mass.

Nurture and formalize a design:

___ Implement actions that address systems issues.

___ Use a process to select appropriate metrics.

___ Conduct a risk assessment.

___ Use a variety of implementation and planning tools.

Guide implementation:

___ Foster collaboration between diverse groups.

___ Utilize organizational politics positively.

___ Identify motivational factors for various individuals.

___ Use short-term gains to build momentum.

___ Coordinate numerous and varied activities ensuring that timelines are met.

Evaluate and institutionalize the change:

___ Create a process to evaluate the change effort.

___ Identify ways to institutionalize the change.

___ Compare the organizational culture to the change results.

___ Create a change-ready organization.

Worksheet 4-1. Organizational Change Readiness Audit

Past change efforts and results:

- In what past change effort have you been involved?
- What do you remember about each change effort:
  - —What happened? Why?
  - —When did this occur?
  - —What were the results?
- How could the change efforts of the past been more successful?
- What would you have done differently?
- What lessons were learned from past change efforts?

Current readiness for change:

- How would you describe the current culture and its readiness to make a change?
- What change efforts are you aware of that are occurring now? Please describe them:
  - —What specifically is happening?
  - —Why is the change occurring?
  - —Is there anything special about the timing?
  - —Who is responsible for the change?
  - —How would you describe employees' willingness to change?
- What barriers exist that will prevent change from occurring, e.g., lack of resources, lack of leadership, dysfunctional culture, rewarded for the wrong thing, policies, procedures, labor agreements, access to the workforce?
- How quickly do employees adjust to changes? Why?
- What must occur for the anticipated change effort to succeed?
- Who should lead the anticipated change effort? Why?
- Who should be involved in this change effort?
- What is the best time to initiate this change?
- What metrics shall we use to measure results?
- What resources are required?
- How would you like to be involved?
- How will we know we have been successful?
- What is the best way to celebrate success?
- What should I have asked, but didn't?

Worksheet 4-2. Change Readiness Predictor

Indicate the degree to which each of the dimensions is a concern to you with regard to your organization's change readiness. Circle the number under the appropriate heading for each factor. Dimensions have been scaled according to their relative importance in predicting the receptivity to change. Total the scores for an overall change readiness index.

	Degree of Concern				
Dimension	**No**	**Little**	**Moderate**	**Substantial**	**Critical**
Comprehensive variables:					
Size of change	4	3	2	1	0
Current internal stress	4	3	2	1	0
External impact	4	3	2	1	0
Change history	4	3	2	1	0
Supportive culture	4	3	2	1	0
Clear internal processes	4	3	2	1	0
Resources:					
Access to workforce	8	6	4	2	0
Workforce flexibility/agility	8	6	4	2	0
Unions/other constraints	8	6	4	2	0
Time commitment	8	6	4	2	0
Money available	8	6	4	2	0
Employee considerations:					
Workforce talent	12	9	6	3	0
Executive leadership	12	9	6	3	0
Skilled change agents	12	9	6	3	0
Management support	12	9	6	3	0
Total the scores for all dimensions:					

Total all columns: __________

If the total change readiness score is: less than 50, conduct crisis intervention before beginning; if it is between 50 and 69, proceed with caution, taking all steps in the process to ensure success; if it is greater than 69, the organization is ready for the planned change.

Source: ebb associates inc, 2004.

Worksheet 4-3. Business Case Template

Remember: A business case should include what is necessary to include—no more, no less. This template may be more (or less) than what you need for an initial business case presentation.

I. Cover Page

Include the change name, date, version if appropriate.

II. Executive Summary

Provide a concise summary of the key highlights. Although located at the front of the document, it is written last. It should be no more than two pages that stand alone as a single source of the overall project purpose, goals, proposed actions, cost/benefits, risks, and success criteria.

III. Current Situation

Present an introduction to the business case analysis to:

A. Provide rationale/purpose of the business case
B. Identify the sponsor
C. Describe the problem or opportunity
D. Describe the current situation
E. Include relevant data and analysis of the options.

IV. Project Description

Provide the objective, a clear definition of what the change will accomplish. Explain how the change will address the business problem/opportunity identified in III. Include:

A. Measurable goals and objectives (ensuring they support the business needs)
B. Performance measures that will be used to determine outcomes
C. Assumptions and how they were arrived
D. Proposed new environment
E. Major effort milestone dates.

V. Environmental Analysis and Alternatives

Describe pertinent current events outside the organization, discuss what other organizations have done, and propose viable options.

VI. Business and Operational Impact

Identify the impact for each stakeholder and technology assessment.

A. Business impact such as a change in service or products provided, or focus or direction of a department
B. Operational impact such as staff training required or reduction of resources
C. Technology requirements.

VII. Preliminary Risk Assessment

Optional at the early stages of a change effort, but if included it identifies the potential risks, assesses risk for impact and probability, and presents a mitigation plan for each risk.

VIII. Cost/Benefit Analysis

Evaluate the costs and benefits associated with each viable alternative.

Worksheet 4-3. Business Case Template (continued)

IX. Implementation Timeline and Strategy

Define the scope of the effort that may include:

A. Project management controls
B. Analysis, development, and design
C. Transitions and training
D. Resources required and from where.

X. Conclusion and Final Recommendations

Provide a selected alternative based on an overall evaluation in terms of impact, risk, and cost/benefit. Next steps are also usually included.

Worksheet 5-1. Sample Team Charter

Team: Talent Resourcing Team Charter

Team Lead: Dr. Frank Carr

Purpose: Address the following Human Capital Strategy Team recommendations:

- Ensure that all team results/recommendations match the greater organizational Human Capital Strategy requirements.
- Align recruitment strategies with workforce planning efforts to close critical position gaps and to employ a diverse workforce.
- Modify the internal recruitment process to eliminate gaps caused by late initiation of the hiring process.
- Educate the organization's leadership about HR flexibilities.
- Develop a succession planning process that
  —holds leaders accountable
  —identifies 25 to 50 key positions requiring a succession plans
  —identifies governance and management responsibilities
  —creates developmental opportunities that prepare employees to compete for key positions.
- Integrate diversity into the overall recruitment and succession plans.

Anticipated deliverables and products:

- Plan and timeline to modify the recruitment process.
- Set of options for increasing diversity in the recruitment and succession plans.
- Define and initiate the succession planning process.
- Communication plan to inform leadership.

Findings from Strategy Team:

- Organization lacks workforce planning and processes.
- Forty-six percent of the current workforce can retire in the next five years.
- The average age of the workforce is 49.29 (up from 48.75 in three years).
- Workforce is not representative of the nation's diversity.
- Processes related to recruitment and hiring are cumbersome and time consuming
- There is very little turnover. Most managers believe the hiring process takes too long and would like more help in identifying and marketing to a more diverse set of prospective candidates.
- Nearly 90 percent of organizations worldwide reported that succession management was a top corporate priority this past year.
- Over half of the organizations interviewed implement a Corporate Management Development Program focusing on formal training for managers including succession planning.

Conclusions:

- Organization's ability to identify workforce imbalances is inadequate.
- National pipelines of talent are shrinking.
- Duplication and a lack of connection exist among the many education and recruitment programs within our offices and our sister organizations.
- Coordinated and integrated recruiting programs and career development with cross-cutting career paths will benefit the enterprise.
- Branding career opportunities for the enterprise could position it as "employer of choice" and increase the enterprise's ability to compete for high talent.

Worksheet 5-1. Sample Team Charter (continued)

Team competencies required:

- Basic understanding of the hiring process
- Experience with the recruitment and hiring process
- Understands the critical need for a succession planning process
- Respected leaders (formal and informal)
- Excellent communication skills
- Inspires high team performance
- Creative, innovative, risk taker
- Viewed as a progressive thought leader
- Results oriented, strategic thinker
- Analytical skills
- Positive attitude.

Team members:

Scott Blacks (finance)
Maggie Masters (HR)
John Connally (contracts)
Leila Ramirez (global)
Tom Paluszkiewicz (research)
Preston Grant (S&T)
Janet Johnshoy (legal)

Guidance:

- Meet at least biweekly for 3–4 hours.
- Preliminary report due on November 7.
- Team Leader Progress Meetings will be held biweekly.
- Final implementation plan due on December 7.
- Obtain commitment from Human Resources, Contracts, and Finance.
- Facilitation will be provided by ebb associates.

______________________________ CEO

______________ Date

Worksheet 5-2. Communication Plan Template

Date	Targeted Audience	Message/Event	Method/Media	Delivery	Status
2/7	Administrative officers	What do performance goals mean to me?	Brown bag lunch	Talent manager	Complete
3/9	All	Why competencies are important to all of us	Podcast	CEO presents; HR designs	Designed and approved; ready for delivery
Monday at 9 a.m. Weekly	Managers	Weekly phone call with leadership for updates	Conference call	Change facilitator/ implementation team	Ongoing
Thursdays, 1:00-3:30	All	Answer questions within department	30-minute listening Posts	Implementation team member	Ongoing

Worksheet 9-1. Evaluate for Impact

Change Intervention Goals	Successful? Why or Why Not?	Contingency Steps

Worksheet 9-2. Evaluate the Change

Event or Action	Failed Miserably	Somewhat Successful	Completely Successful
A solid rationale for change was provided			
Costs were predicted and an adequate ROI was determined			
The leaders of the change were willing volunteers			
A shared vision was created			
Commitment to change was created			
Everyone who wanted to be involved had an opportunity			
The right people were selected for the teams			
A comprehensive implementation plan for the change was prepared			
The change focused on results not activities			
Changes were completed with a minimum of interruption to the workforce			
Customers experienced no interruption of services			
Employees received training, development, and coaching as needed			
The change can be linked directly with the organizational strategic plan			
Monitoring and adjusting occurred in response to problems in the process			
Progress was tracked and published			
Clear success metrics were identified			
Change has been institutionalized with formal policies, systems, and structures			
Top management is committed to continued success of the change			
Employees are pleased with the results			

Worksheet 9-3. Lessons Learned for Leaders

Review each of these statements and rate them in the first column using the following scale (and numbers in between): 0 = not at all—must have forgotten; 3 = pretty darn average and I need improvement; 6 = completely—didn't miss a beat.

Add your comments in the third column.

To what extent did you:

0–6	Skills and Behaviors	Comments
	Provide information early and often to employees?	
	Model behavior expected of others?	
	Clearly explain the reason for the change?	
	Focus on results?	
	Help employees understand what's in it for them?	
	Build a team trusted by the organization?	
	Set expectations for continuous change?	
	Create stories and paint a future vision?	
	Engineer some quick wins?	
	Encourage others to participate?	
	Listen to individuals for facts and feelings?	
	Provide all resources required?	
	Give others credit?	
	Provide recognition for small and large wins?	
	Continue to be upbeat and positive?	
	Help to address resistance?	
	Empathize with others' needs and concerns?	
	Manage the transition effectively?	
	Identify ways to symbolize the new identity?	
	Address the change from a systems approach?	
	Find ways to celebrate?	
	Participate in the evaluation?	

What strengths do you think you displayed during the change effort?

About the Author

Elaine Biech is the president and managing principal of ebb associates inc, an organizational development firm that helps organizations work through large-scale change. She has been in the training and consulting field for 30 years, working with many leading business, government, and nonprofit organizations. She specializes in helping people work as teams to maximize their effectiveness. Customizing all her work for individual clients, she conducts strategic planning sessions and implements organization-wide systems for initiatives such as improving quality, reengineering operational processes, and mentoring.

Biech has written or edited more than four dozen books and articles, including *The Business of Consulting*, 2nd edition, 2007; *90 World-Class Activities by 90 World-Class Trainers*, 2007; the nine-volume set of ASTD *Certification Study Guides*, 2006; "12 Habits of Successful Trainers," ASTD *Infoline*, 2005; *The ASTD Infoline Dictionary of Basic Trainer Terms*, 2005; *Training for Dummies*, 2005; *Marketing Your Consulting Services*, 2003; *The Consultant's Quick Start Guide*, 2001; *The Pfeiffer Book of Successful Team-Building Tools*, 2001; *The Consultant's Legal Guide*, 2000; *Interpersonal Skills: Understanding Your Impact on Others*,1996; *Building High Performance*, 1998; and *The ASTD Sourcebook: Creativity and Innovation—Widen Your Spectrum*, 1996. Since 1998, she has served as the consulting editor of both the *Pfeiffer Annual for Consultants* and *Pfeiffer Annual for Trainers*. Her books have been translated into Chinese, German, and Dutch. In addition, she has made presentations at many national and international conferences and has been featured in dozens of publications, including the *Wall Street Journal, Harvard Management Update, Washington Post,* and *Fortune*.

Biech received her B.S. from the University of Wisconsin–Superior in business and education consulting, and her M.S. in human resource development. She is active at the national level of ASTD, serving on the National Conference Design Committee in 1990, as a member of the National ASTD Board of Directors, and as ASTD's secretary from 1991 to 1994. She initiated and chaired the ASTD Consultant's Day for seven years and was the International Conference Design chair in 2000. In addition to her work with ASTD, she has served on the Independent Consultants Association's Advisory Committee and on the Instructional Systems Association Board of Directors. She was the recipient of the 1992 National ASTD Torch Award, the 2004 ASTD Volunteer-Staff Partnership Award, and the 2006 ASTD Gordon M. Bliss Award. She was selected for the 1995 Wisconsin Women Entrepreneur's Mentor Award. In 2001, she received the Instructional Systems Association's highest award, the ISA Spirit Award. She can be reached at ebboffice@aol.com or at www.ebbweb.com.

Index